JSOT/ASOR MONOGRAPH SERIES

4

Editor
Walter E. Aufrecht

JOURNAL FOR THE STUDY OF THE OLD TESTAMENT
SUPPLEMENT SERIES

103

Editors
David J A Clines
Philip R Davies

JSOT Press
Sheffield

The
SOCIOLOGY
of POTTERY in
ANCIENT PALESTINE

The Ceramic Industry and the
Diffusion of Ceramic Style in the
Bronze and Iron Ages

Bryant G. Wood

Journal for the Study of the Old Testament
Supplement Series 103
JSOT/ASOR Monographs 4

To John S. Holladay, Jr,
who posed the question and
provided help along the way

Copyright © 1990 Sheffield Academic Press

Published by JSOT Press

for the American Schools of Oriental Research

JSOT Press is an imprint of
Sheffield Academic Press Ltd
The University of Sheffield
343 Fulwood Road
Sheffield S10 3BP
England

Printed on acid-free paper in Great Britain
by Billing & Sons Ltd
Worcester

British Library Cataloguing in Publication Data available

JSOT/ASOR Monograph Series, 4
JSOT Supplement Series, 103

ISSN 0267-5684
ISSN 0309-0787
ISBN 1-85075-269-9

CONTENTS

TABLES

FIGURES

PREFACE

I was first challenged with the problem of the diffusion of ceramic style in ancient Palestine by my thesis advisor, Professor John S. Holladay, Jr, of the University of Toronto. After six months of diligent research I was able to provide what I believe is a reasonable answer to the question of why ceramic style was similar across Palestine and why that style changed through time in much the same manner in different locations. The results of this research became one chapter in my Ph.D. thesis (Wood 1985:78-220). The present monograph is an expanded version of the original study, which was restricted in scope to the terminal phase of the Late Bronze Age.

Before the problem of the diffusion of ceramic style can be broached, it is first necessary to understand the ceramic industry of ancient Palestine. Thus, the study is divided into two parts: the first dealing with the nature of the ceramic industry and the second dealing with the spatial and temporal diffusion of ceramic style.

I am indebted to Professor Holladay for his guidance and helpful comments during the initial stages of the research. Special thanks go to Rüdiger Vossen of the Hamburgisches Museum für Völkerkunde and Ruben Reina of the University of Pennsylvania for providing illustrations of the transport and sale of ceramics in contemporary cultures. Professor David Clines of Sheffield made many emendations to the final proofs. A number of individuals and institutions were kind enough to grant permission to reproduce copyrighted material for which I am grateful. They are: William Anderson of the University of Pennsylvania, École Biblique et Archéologique Française, Haverford College, Israel Antiquities Authority, the Metropolitan Museum of Art, the University Museum of the University of Pennsylvania and the Wenner–

Gren Foundation for Anthropological Research. I also wish to express my gratitude to my wife Faith for her unwavering support, for her able assistance on several research trips to various libraries and for typing the manuscript.

Harrisburg, Pennsylvania
August 1990

INTRODUCTION

A large part of archaeological research in Palestine is devoted to the excavation, processing, analysis and documentation of pottery. The focus, however, has been almost exclusively on the pottery itself, to the neglect of the sociology of pottery, that is, the relationship between pottery and its cultural and economic environment.[1] This has resulted in a restricted view of the role of ceramics in ancient Palestine and has limited the use of ceramic data in archaeological analyses. In order to make the maximum use of ceramic data, the overall system of pottery making and its related activities must be reconstructed (van der Leeuw 1977:75; Rice 1987:168).

Stanley Casson was one of the earliest, if not the first, Near Eastern scholar to recognize the importance of a sociological approach to the study of pottery:

> Since archaeologists are by nature and origin academic, except for a few rare spirits ... they tend to create from the material archaeological remains which they study a world which, here and there, may be ever so little out of touch with reality. In the study of ceramics this is especially evident. The survival of pots and potsherds on ancient sites, and the organization of their study almost into a science, has given an importance to pottery which far exceeds that given to other material ... But one aspect of ceramic seems to me to have received slight attention. I know of almost no literature or research which deals with the *economic* aspect of pot-making (1938:464-65).

1. The methodology of pottery fabrication in ancient Palestine has received considerable attention: Kelso and Thorley 1943; Kelso 1948; Franken 1969, 1971; Hammond 1971; Johnston 1974a, 1986; Glanzman 1983; Edwards and Segnit 1984. These studies, however, do not move beyond the fabrication process itself to ask questions concerning the type of workshop that produced the pottery, the manner in which pottery and pottery styles were diffused throughout the country, the use of pottery in a typical household, etc.

Casson also realized the potential of ethnographic research for properly understanding the role of pottery in antiquity (1938:473).

In the recent past there has been an increased awareness of the importance of the sociology of pottery.[1] Frederick Matson, one of the pioneers in this area, has stressed the need for a better understanding of the cultural context in which ceramics were made and used, otherwise 'they form a sterile record of limited worth' (1965:202; cf. 1972:212; Rice 1987:168).

In this two-part study, I shall attempt to reconstruct the sociological system in which pottery functioned in the Bronze and Iron Ages in Palestine. In Part I the industry itself will be examined: the technology of the potters, which will give insight into who was practicing pottery making and for what purpose, the organization of the potters, and the spatial distribution of the craft. In Part II I shall take up the complex matter of the diffusion of ceramic style.

Both archaeological and ethnographic data are utilized in the study. Properly used, ethnographic analogy is the most viable means of gaining insight into practices of the past (Schiffer 1978:239; Binford 1983:23-24, 104; Wylie 1985:107). There are two types of ethnographic analogy: continuous and discontinuous. In continuous analogy, the phenomenon being studied can be linked to the past by an unbroken tradition which has continued since antiquity. In areas where this is not the case, analogies from other regions which have similar ecological, environmental and cultural characteristics ('discontinuous' analogies) may be utilized (Binford 1967:2-3; Gould 1978:255; 1980:55-56).

Realizing the value of ethnographic data, and that traditional workshops are fast disappearing in the face of encroaching technology, ethnographers have produced a plethora of studies on traditional pottery making in recent

1. For informative studies on the sociology of pottery in contemporary cultures, see especially the work of Foster at Tzintzuntzan, Mexico (1960, 1965), David and Hennig at Bé in North Cameroon (1972), Reina and Hill in Guatemala (1978), Haaland at Darfur in western Sudan (1978) and Crossland and Posnausky at Begho in Ghana (1978). For an overview, see Rice 1987:168-206.

years.[1] In Palestine today, the craft of pottery making is vastly different from what it was in the Bronze and Iron Ages. As we shall see, pottery production in antiquity was a full-time craft specialization utilizing potters' wheels and permanent kilns and practiced by men. Although there are some remnants of the ancient traditions still being practiced in isolated instances, pottery making in modern-day Palestine is largely either an up-to-date operation using electric wheels and kilns or a part-time activity carried on by village women using primitive techniques. Ethnographic studies conducted in Palestine, therefore, are of limited value in reconstructing the sophisticated ceramic industry that was in operation in the large city-states of the Bronze and Iron Ages. We are thus obliged to use discontinuous analogies in investigating the sociology of pottery in ancient Palestine.[2] Happily, in other Mediterranean lands (e.g. Egypt, North Africa, Greece, Spain) ceramic production, distribution and use continue today in some areas much as they did in antiquity, providing ethnographic analogies which can be applied to Palestine.

Sufficient ethnographic studies have been conducted in various parts of the world to demonstrate that there are cross-cultural generalizations concerning the relationship of ceramics to environment and culture (see particularly Arnold 1985; van der Leeuw 1977). Since these generalizations are universal in nature they apply to the past as well as the present (Arnold 1985:ix-x, 14-16). It is therefore methodologically correct and, in fact, imperative, to use ethnographic analogies

1. For a review of this literature, see Kramer 1985; Rice 1987:113-67.
2. Ethnographic studies on the sociology of pottery in the Middle East are sadly lacking. On the methods of fabricating traditional pottery in the Levant, which include some sociological data, see the following: Palestine—Einsler 1914; Crowfoot 1932, 1938 (all three conveniently summarized by Glock, 1982:146-47); Glock 1983:175-77; Bresenham 1985; Mersehn 1985; Lebanon—Hankey 1968; Cyprus—Taylor and Tufnell 1930; Hampe and Winter 1962; Johnston 1974b; Yon 1981, 1985; London 1987a, 1987b; 1989; London, Egoumenidou and Karageorghis 1989; Egypt—Randall-Maciver 1905; Brissaud 1982; Nicholson and Patterson 1985a, 1985b. For the Aegean, see Xanthoudides 1927; Casson 1938, 1951; Hampe and Winter 1962, 1965; Matson 1972: 211-23; 1973; Voyatzoglou 1973, 1974; Guest-Papamanoli 1983. For Morocco, see Vossen and Ebert 1986; for Iraq, see Ochsenschlager 1974.

14   *The Sociology of Pottery*

not only from the Mediterranean area, but from other parts of
the world as well, to interpret archaeological data from Palestine. By bringing together these two bodies of information,
namely the archaeological and the ethnographic, a rather
complete picture of the ceramic industry and the day-to-day
usage of pottery in ancient Palestine is obtained (van der
Leeuw 1977:75).[1]

Our methodology throughout will be first to examine the
archaeological data concerning the particular aspect of
ceramics under investigation. Secondly, we shall appeal to
ethnographic evidence from cultures still making and using
pottery for utilitarian purposes to interpret and supplement
the archaeological data. From a synthesis of these data, two
hypotheses will be offered concerning the role of ceramics in
the Bronze and Iron Ages in Palestine: one to explain the
commercial manufacturing–distribution system and one to
explain temporal style change.

1. For an example of how archaeological and ethnographic information can be combined to reconstruct an ancient ceramic industry, see
Peacock 1982.

PART I

THE NATURE OF THE CERAMIC INDUSTRY

> So with the potter sitting at his labor, revolving the wheel with
> his feet. He is always concerned for his products, and turns
> them out in quantity. With his hands he molds the clay, and
> with his feet softens it. His care is for proper coloring, and he
> keeps watch on the fire of his kiln (Ecclus 38.29-30).

We possess more information about the pottery industry than
any other ancient industry of Palestine. Not only do we have
abundant, even overwhelming, remains of the almost inde-
structible products of this industry, but we also have remnants
of the manufacturing process itself—parts of potters' wheels
and other tools, kilns, and, in some cases, nearly complete
workshops.[1] From nearby cultures we also have pictorial data
depicting the pottery manufacturing process in antiquity.[2] In
addition to this wealth of archaeological data, we have living
testimony concerning the manufacture, distribution and
functional use of ceramic wares in nearby contemporary pre-
industrial cultures. Many of these cultures are carrying on
ceramic traditions which have continued unbroken from
antiquity (Guest-Papamanoli 1983; Johnston 1984:81-82).

Evidence for Mass Production

In evaluating the sociology of pottery, a necessary first question is 'How are the pots produced?' Are the vessels individu-

---

1. These data have not been systematically studied for Palestine. For
an examination of the Egyptian evidence, see Holthoer 1977:5-40 (cf.
Bourriau 1981:14-23; Hope 1982:18-22); for the Mesopotamian evidence,
see Barralet 1968.
2. For ancient Egypt, see Holthoer 1977; Killebrew 1982. For ancient
Greece, see Noble 1965.

ally produced by hand for family use or are they mass produced for commercial sale with the aid of a mechanical device,
namely a potter's wheel? In the Bronze and Iron Ages in
Palestine, the evidence overwhelmingly points to mass production. When one encounters a large group of obviously contemporary vessels, say from a well-sealed destruction deposit
or a tomb of limited time range, one is struck by the fact that
vessels of the same type are nearly identical in their morphological characteristics. Such uniformity, notes Holladay, is 'a
characteristic of sealed, simultaneously destroyed deposits in
general' (1976:255). Large numbers of like artifacts in standard sizes and limited taxonomy suggest mass production
(Kelso and Thorley 1943:120; Rice 1981:220). This deduction is
verified by the quantities of identical vessels found in and
around ancient kilns and other, more indirect, evidence
recovered in archaeological excavations.

At Hazor, in Area H, a potters' kiln was found outside the
entrance to a LB IB temple. Inside the kiln were 20 nearly
identical miniature votive bowls, as well as a number of larger
bowls and a miniature goblet (Yadin 1972:82; Yadin *et al.* 1989:
230). A similar find was made at Deir el-Balaḥ, where a small
kiln dating to the LB IIB period was found which contained
votive bowls (T. Dothan 1981:129). During the Late Bronze
and Iron Ages, the entire east slope of Megiddo was devoted to
the pottery industry, with the many caves located there being
utilized as potters' workshops (see p. 40 below). One of the
many kilns, No. 22, dating to the Iron II period, contained 30
poorly fired jar stands (Guy 1938:77). A large group of hole-
mouth jars was found adjacent to Kiln 33, also from the Iron II
period (1938:81). In the vicinity of an Iron II kiln at Tell en-
Naṣbeh, a large deposit of store jar fragments was found (Badè
1928:28). In another Iron II kiln at Ashdod, a quantity of hole-
mouth jars was discovered (M. Dothan 1971:92) and in the
same area a Hellenistic kiln contained a group of identical
bowls (1971:118).

These finds indicate that ceramic wares in ancient Palestine
were mass produced in an assembly-line process, with batches
of identical vessels being fabricated together. In addition, the
presence of potters' wheels and permanent kilns (see below)
are strong indicators of a large-scale commercial operation

(Ehrich 1965:9; Scott 1965:392; Peacock 1982:25; van der Leeuw 1984:59).

Some rather unusual data testifying to the presence of an organized pottery industry which produced large numbers of vessels was recently discovered at Lachish. The excavator describes the items as 'sausage- or cigar-shaped clay objects' and he states that 'the function of the clay objects remains obscure for the present' (Ussishkin 1978:74, 76). They are c. 2.6–2.7 cm in diameter and c. 9-12 cm in length. Approximately 278 of them were found. Ussishkin's description of the artifacts suggests a possible explanation for their use: 'the potter took a piece of clay and rolled it into shape, as if he were preparing pastry rolls' (1978:74).

These objects which at first seem so puzzling appear to be nothing more than the coils which the potters prepared in anticipation of making coil-built vessels. Often large numbers of these coils were made in advance and stored in preparation for a production run of coil-built vessels (see, conveniently, Yon 1981:88).[1]

As a rule, such objects would not survive to be discovered by the archaeologist since they were utilized very soon after they were rolled. If, on the other hand, the coils were never fabricated into vessels, they would normally become an indistinguishable part of the general debris since they were made of unfired clay. Most of the Lachish coils were found in constructional fills for the podium of the Level IV palace-fort. A number were found on the floors and in the debris layers of Level VI in Area S as well, prompting Ussishkin to conclude that 'they date to Level VI, or possibly even earlier' (1983:154). If they originated in Level VI, this would explain how the coils came to be preserved. The Level VI city was engulfed in a great conflagration[2] which would have effectively baked any unfired clay objects.[3]

1. On coil building in general, see Franken 1969:89-90; Johnston 1974a:92-95.
2. For the evidence, see Tufnell, Inge and Harding 1940:20; Isserlin and Tufnell 1950:82; Tufnell 1953:77; Aharoni 1975:12; Clamer and Ussishkin 1977:71; Ussishkin 1978:10, 45, 92; 1983:114, 116, 120, 168.
3. Ussishkin, however, believes the coils were intentionally fired in a kiln (personal communication, January 31, 1985). Wright's suggestion

18 *The Sociology of Pottery*

An urban society in antiquity required large quantities of ceramic ware because of its common usage, its fragile nature and its removal from circulation by use in burials and other cultic activities (Arnold 1985:127-67). The advantages of mass production in such a high-demand market have been pointed out by Rathje (1975:430). Cheap and efficient production of large quantities of pottery is made possible by standardization, simplification and specialization. Since each specialist becomes an expert in his specific task, the products attain a technical superiority over those produced by non-specialists. Routinization of production also minimizes loss due to technical error. Shipping becomes easier and loss through breakage is reduced when standardized shapes and sizes are produced. Overall, mass production results in increased output and distribution per unit of labor and material.

The Potter's Wheel

It is generally agreed, based on visual examination of characteristic sherds and whole pieces, that in the MB II period (c. 2000 BCE) Palestinian pottery was 'thrown' on a fast wheel (Kelso and Thorley 1943:96; Amiran 1969:90; Franken 1969:80, 92; Dever 1976:7, 8; Johnston 1977:206); that is, it was made on a wheel spinning fast enough so that the centrifugal force formed the vessel, with the potter merely guiding the clay with his hands to attain the desired shape.[1] This technology apparently was lost in the Late Bronze Age, but was regained in the Iron II period (Kelso and Thorley 1943:93; Franken 1969:92; 1971:234; Bienkowski 1986:10; cf. Glanzman 1983). Stone bearings from potters' wheels have been found in abundance throughout Palestine, from the Early

(1983) that the coils were used as 'kiln hangers' lacks persuasive force. The cited parallels are associated with the production of Islamic glazed ware in the Medieval period and are much larger in size than the Lachish examples. No such hanger pegs have been found in the numerous Bronze and Iron Age kilns excavated in Palestine.

1. On potters' wheels in general, see Foster 1959; H. Hodges 1964:28-33; Childe 1965; Nicklin 1971:35-38; Holthoer 1977:31-32; Johnston 1977; Loebert 1984:205-12.

Bronze period onward (figs. 1, 2).[1] From the archaeological evidence and ethnographic examples it is posible to reconstruct the potter's wheel of antiquity.

The stone bearings from potters' wheels found in Palestine, referred to as 'potters' wheels' in excavation reports, are of various sizes, but invariably consist of one or both of two components: (1) a lower whorl with a cavity, or socket, in the center, and (2) an upper whorl with a projection, or tenon, in the center. The two whorls fit together, with the tenon mating the socket. From the wear marks on such whorls, it is evident that the upper whorl (sometimes called a 'pivot') rotated on the lower whorl. In reality, these stone whorls are thrust bearings from a more elaborate apparatus made of wood. The stone bearings were used in the so-called 'fast' potter's wheel, which was of two types, the single wheel and the double wheel.

The Single Wheel

In the single or simple wheel (also called a 'hand wheel'), the lower bearing is secured in the ground or on a platform or bench. A wooden disc (called a 'flywheel', 'wheel head', 'table', or 'platform') is attached to the upper bearing[2] and the assembly is placed on the lower bearing with the tenon inserted in the socket. The wooden disc is then rotated by hand by an assistant while the potter fashions his vessels. The tenon in the upper bearing acts to keep the wooden disc centered and running true. The lower portion of the potter's wheel shown in

1. Stone wheels from the Early Bronze Age and the beginning of the Middle Bronze Age may be from simple tournettes. Other examples of potter's wheel thrust bearings, in addition to those shown in figs. 1 and 2 are: Early Bronze Age—Kh. el-Kerak (Maisler, Stekelis and Avi-Yonah 1952:170); Middle Bronze Age—Tell el-Ajjul (Petrie 1931:11, pl. 52:10); Late Bronze Age—Tell el-Ajjul (Petrie 1952:18, pls. 20:48-50); Iron Age II—Tell en-Nasbeh (McCown 1947:258, pl. 100:6); date unknown—Gezer (Macalister 1912, 2: figs. 228, 229); provenance unknown—Bliss and Macalister 1902:143, pl. 73:9; Amiran and Shenhav 1984:112 n. 1, fig. 1. Similar evidence has been found in Egypt (Hope 1981, 1982).

2. A Byzantine upper bearing from Mefalsim had traces of iron rust on it, suggesting that the flywheel may have been attached by means of an iron band (Amiran and Shenhav 1984:108).

fig. 3, without the shaft or upper wheel, is, in effect, a single potter's wheel.[1]

Archaeological Evidence. In the LB IIA potters' workshop at Hazor (p. 35 below) a platform or work bench was found, c. 1.5 × 1.0 m and 40 cm high, made of field stones (fig. 12, Room 6225). On top of the platform was a complete thrust bearing assembly (fig. 1.9). The bearing assembly undoubtedly belonged to a single-wheel type of potter's wheel. A double wheel would not have been placed on such a bench whereas an elevation of 40 cm is a comfortable working height for a single potter's wheel, assuming that the potter was sitting on a low stool. A single wheel being used by an 18th Dynasty Egyptian potter is seen in fig. 11.[2]

Ethnographic Evidence. Matson has observed the use of the single wheel in Afghanistan and notes that it is extensively used in India (1974:346; cf. Saraswati 1979:16-19). In these eastern countries it is turned with a stick (Johnston 1977:197-207). The potters of Crete use a modified version of the single wheel to fabricate pithoi. It has a short wooden axle with a wooden disc at the top where the pithos is worked and an iron point at the bottom which rotates in a socket of stone or metal. The axle is held steady by a horizontal beam, and a short wooden bar which passes through the lower end of the axle is used by the potter's assistant to turn the wheel (Xanthoudides 1927:123, pls. 20b and 21).

The Double Wheel
The second type of fast wheel is the double or compound wheel (also called a 'combined wheel', 'foot wheel' or 'kick wheel'). In this type a wooden disc (the 'flywheel') is attached to the upper bearing as with the simple wheel, but now a vertical shaft is attached to the center of the wooden disc. At the end of the shaft is a second, smaller, wooden disc (the 'wheel-head',

1. For experimental reconstruction of single potters' wheels, see Amiran and Shenhav 1984: fig. 3; Edwards and Jacobs 1986.
2. For additional pictorial evidence showing the various designs of the single wheel in ancient Egypt, see Holthoer 1977:31-33.

'working platform' or 'table') where the vessel is fashioned
(fig. 3). The shaft is steadied by a horizontal wooden bar with a
hole in it, through which the shaft passes. Since the potter can
now rotate the wheel by kicking the lower disc with his foot, an
assistant is no longer needed (Foster 1959:104; Childe
1965:201; Nicklin 1971:35-38; Holthoer 1977:31).[1]

Archaeological Evidence. In an early Iron I potters' cave at
Lachish (pp. 35-36 below), two pits were found which appear
to be emplacements for potters' wheels (fig. 14). One, Pit C, is
near the entrance to the cave and has a stone seat at the edge
of the pit. Unfortunately, the Lachish publication does not
provide precise dimensions for the installation, except to say
that it was 'irregular' and 'about a metre deep' (Tufnell *et al.*
1958:292). From the photo (1958:pl. 8.2) it appears that the 1
m dimension was taken from the bottom of the stone seat,
which itself is c. 50 cm thick. It is an ideal arrangement for a
potter's wheel since above the stone seat is a ventilation shaft
admitting light and air. Inasmuch as Pit C appears to be too
low in comparison with the height of the seat for a single
wheel to be effectively utilized, it most likely accommodated a
double wheel.

There can be little doubt that Pit D located further back in
the Lachish cave was fashioned to house a potter's wheel.
Again, precise information is lacking in the Lachish publication. Pit D is c. 60 cm in diameter (1958:pls. 8.4 and 92), with a
smaller hole c. 30 cm in diameter (1958:292) centered at its
bottom. The lower hole would have made an excellent receptacle for a lower thrust bearing (the two upper bearings found
in the cave [figs. 2.1, 2.2] are 19 and 16 cm in diameter, respectively). The upper, larger diameter, section of the pit would
then have accommodated a flywheel attached to an upper

1. This reconstruction is based on modern potters' wheels in the
Middle East (see below). Other designs using metal and wood may
have been in use in Palestine in antiquity, but we have no evidence to
indicate what these designs might have been. In Jer. 18.3 (c. 6th century BCE) the potter's wheel is mentioned (*'obnayim*). The word is in
the dual and literally means 'pair of stones'. The name may derive
from the fact that the earliest potters' wheels were possibly tournettes
comprised of a pair of stones (p. 19 n. 1, cf. Kelso 1948:9).

bearing. Such an arrangement would have been practical only for a double wheel, since it would have been very awkward for an assistant to turn a single wheel by hand if it were housed in a pit. A double wheel, on the other hand, could easily have been foot-operated by a potter on a stool at the edge of the pit, since the top of the flywheel would have been approximately flush with the floor. If this were the case, the size of the pit suggests a flywheel diameter of c. 60 cm.[1]

In Cave 37 at Megiddo, dating to the Iron II period, a potter's wheel emplacement (Pit H, fig. 4) was found which is very similar to Pit D in the Lachish potters' cave. Located near the entrance to the cave, the diameter of the upper part of the pit is c. 1 m. Centered at the bottom of the pit is a smaller hole c. 60 cm in diameter. The overall depth of the pit is c. 40 cm, while the depth of the upper, larger diameter, portion of the pit is c. 10 cm. At the bottom of the pit was 'a worn stone socket' (Guy 1938:80), undoubtedly the lower thrust bearing from a potter's wheel. Such an emplacement would have accommodated a somewhat larger potter's wheel than Pit D at Lachish, with the flywheel being some 1 m in diameter.

From an examination of the pottery itself, it appears that the fast wheel was in use at least as early as the MB II period in Palestine. The potter's wheel emplacements in Cave 4034 at Lachish and Cave 37 at Megiddo provide archaeological evidence that the double wheel was in use at least by the beginning of the Iron I period and was also in use in the Iron II period.[2]

Ethnographic Evidence. Childe describes contemporary potters' wheels in Palestine which use the same type of stone bearings as have been found at ancient sites (1965:201). As in ancient Palestine, Childe notes that the lower bearing is placed in a pit. The same practice has been observed in Deir el-Gharbi, Egypt (Nicholson and Patterson 1985a:58), and on the island of Djerba, off the coast of Tunisia (Johnston 1984:85).

1. Amiran and Shenhav found that a flywheel diameter of 60 cm is adequate for throwing vessels (1984:108).
2. Pictorial evidence indicates that the double wheel was not used in Egypt until the Persian Period (Holthoer 1977:32).

Holthoer also details the construction of modern potters' wheels in Egypt (1977:31; cf. Peacock 1982:28).

Much the same type of wheel is used by the potters in Beit Shabab, Lebanon. The lower wheel is either a heavy stone or wooden disc which revolves on a fixed pivot. Attached to the disc is a vertical axle which is socketed to the underside of the round table on which the pot is thrown. The potter stands as he works and kicks the wheel counterclockwise; he has no stool or support for his body. Hankey notes that this type is used throughout the Mediterranean region (1968:28, pls. VIII, XIIB and XIIIA).

In addition to the single wheel, the potters of Crete also use a double wheel (Xanthoudides 1927:121-22, pl. XXa). It is constructed of a lower flywheel of wood which has an axle passing through it. At the lower end of the axle is an iron pin which acts as a pivot; it is set in a hole in a small slab of hard stone or metal anchored in the ground. At the top end of the axle is a smaller wooden disc which serves as the working platform. The axle passes through a hole in a horizontal plank which holds the wheel steady and prevents oscillations. Each time a vessel is formed, a pottery disc is secured to the upper wooden disc with clay and the work is done on the disc. Similar pottery discs have been found on Minoan sites and part of one was found in Cave 63 at Megiddo (Guy 1938: pl. 158.19).[1]

With regard to the operation of the traditional potter's wheel, Matson observes that most village wheels wobble considerably, compelling the potter to adjust his forming techniques and rhythm to the idiosyncrasies of his wheel (1972:215). Matson observed one wheel in Vounaria, Greece, which was said to be 100 years old (1972:214).

Studies of potters in various parts of the world have shown that the potter's wheel is used almost exclusively by men, while women produce hand-made vessels (Foster 1959:109; Scott 1965:407; Johnston 1974a:95; Reina and Hill 1978:21;

---

1. Other potters' wheels are pictured in Johnston 1974a: figs. 9 (Afghanistan = Johnston 1986:919), 10 (location not stated); cf. Johnston 1977; Yon 1981: figs. 170, 423 (Ibn Hani, Syria); Matson 1972: pls. 15-2, 15-3 (Vounaria, Greece). For sketches of modern wheels, see Hampe and Winter 1962:17; Voyatzoglou 1973, reproduced in Peacock 1982: fig. 9.2; Nicholson and Patterson 1985b: fig. 4 (=1985a:55).

24   *The Sociology of Pottery*

Kramer 1985:79). It has been suggested that this is because more strength and continuous energy are required to operate a fast wheel than a simple tournette (Foster 1959:116-17; cf. Nicholson and Patterson 1985b:225) or that mechanical devices belong in the realm of men (Johnston 1977:206). Kramer, however, is probably correct in rejecting these views as overly simplified and maintaining that much more complex social relationships are involved (1985:79). Arnold discusses these relationships in detail (1985:99-108, 225-31).

Where pottery making is a part-time, seasonal activity, it is confined to the home. Since females are closely attached to the household, while males are involved in subsistence activities outside the home, females are normally involved in pottery making in this situation (1985:100-105). Because pottery making is not a full-time subsistence activity in this case and is done in conjunction with other household chores, it remains a low-output operation characterized by hand-forming and open firing (van der Leeuw 1977:70-72; Arnold 1985:226).

When pottery making becomes a full-time occupation, usually as a result of population pressure, the potters are males since it is now a subsistence activity (Arnold 1985:106-108; 227-28). Technical innovations such as wheels, drying sheds and kilns become necessary to provide sufficient output for subsistence and also to reduce the risk of loss (Arnold 1985:228). Since the potter's wheel is associated with a full-time subsistence activity, the wheel is invariably operated by a male. It safely can be assumed, therefore, that the large majority of potters in Bronze and Iron Age Palestine were male.

Through a study of the pottery of Deir 'Allā and other sites, Franken has argued that the art of throwing vessels was lost in the Late Bronze Age, since in the Iron I period the vessels were made by hand with a mold or by coiling (Franken 1969:88-94; 1971:234).[1] Similarly, Bienkowski has concluded

1. In the Baq'ah Valley, c. 25 km from Deir 'Allā, Glanzman has found that thin-walled bowls were turned on a wheel in the Iron I period, whereas they were coil-built in the LB II period (1983: table 1); cf. Glanzman and Fleming 1986; McGovern 1986:37-45.

that at Jericho Late Bronze Age pots were turned on a much slower wheel than Middle Bronze Age vessels (1986:10).

Foster has studied the use of the 'fast' wheel by potters in various parts of the world and concludes that the potential of the wheel for throwing pots is rarely exploited (1959:101; cf. Nicklin 1971:35-36). Many times, Foster observes, the wheel simply is used as a turntable rather than for throwing a pot (1959:109). This may have been the case in the Late Bronze and Iron I period. The technology was available, but the skill had been lost—possibly one of the many side effects of the distintegration of the urbanized city-state system in Palestine.

Miscellaneous Fabrication Equipment

Potters' Jars

In addition to potters' wheel thrust bearings, there are a number of other artifacts related to pottery fabrication. Tufnell was the first to recognize 'potters' jars' as a distinctive class of vessels associated with the potter's craft (Tufnell *et al.* 1958:196). The examples shown in fig. 5 come from contexts which are known from additional evidence to be potters' workshop areas. Such vessels would have been used to contain various liquids related to the manufacture of pottery: water for moistening the clay while turning a vessel, or slip, wash, or paint. In all cases, the vessels have wide mouths, making the contents easily accessible by dipping a rag, brush, or hand into the vessel.

Hand Tools

Another tool commonly found in pottery shops is the forming tool. The potter would use a sherd, whose edges were worn smooth, to shape and form the sides of the vessel as he was turning it (cf. Anderson 1979:544). Sometimes a hole was drilled in the sherd to serve as a finger grip.[1] Peacock (1982:

---

1. For examples see: Guy 1938: pls. 135, objs. 270-74; 136:17; 138:18; 140, obj. 2794, 34; 154, objs. 14, 15, 53, 54, 57; 155, objs. 3334, 3336, 3347; 156, objs. 1351, 1357; 158:1, 4, objs. 5524, M413, 18, obj. 5527, 20, objs. 3926, 3927; Pritchard 1975: figs. 29:6, 7; Tufnell *et al.* 1958: pl. 49:15; Briend and Jean-Baptiste 1980: pls. 82:7-9. A number of the above are shown in Wood 1985: pl. 3. Other possible examples of forming tools of

figs. 1, 6, 10) illustrates a number of forming tools used by traditional potters today. Shells and smooth stones were used for burnishing (Tufnell *et al.* 1958: pl. 49:15), and ordinary saddle querns and mortars and pestles, usually of basalt, were used for grinding temper and coloring pigments.[1] The large funnels and 'drill sockets' found in the Megiddo potters' caves may also be associated with the potter's craft since they were found exclusively in pottery workshops.[2]

The Kiln

Permanent kilns, as opposed to open firing, were generally used in the Bronze and Iron Ages. The advantages of kiln firing are: greater fuel efficiency (less heat loss), higher temperature and better control of the atmosphere around the pots.[3] In open firing, a proportionately greater amount of fuel is required, temperatures are lower, resulting in poor firing, and the heating is uneven, causing many pots to be lost due to cracking. Two types of kilns were in use: the vertical or updraft kiln and the horizontal or down-draft kiln. The vertical kiln was by far the most frequently used type.

Both the vertical and the horizontal kiln had all the elements of a modern kiln: a fire box where fuel is burned and heat generated,[4] a chamber where the pottery is placed and which retains heat, and a flue or exit from which the spent gases escape. This arrangement creates a draft that pulls air into the fire box, heats it, and moves the hot gases through the

unknown date are: Sellin 1904: fig. 54; Macalister 1912, 3: pls. 24:20; 48; 191:5, 15.

1. Examples found in potters' workshops are: Guy 1938: pls. 135, objs. 101, 104, 107, 609-11; 136:15, 16; 154:10, 14, 15, objs. 6-8, 47, 48, 601-603 (= fig. 127, p. 104), 620, 627, 7103; 157:6, 7; 158:22, 23; Yadin *et al.* 1958: pls. 25:3; 87:23, 25; Yadin *et al.* 1960: pls. 127:16, 19; Tufnell *et al.* 1958:91, pl. 49:14.

2. Examples of funnels are: Guy 1938: pls. 37:13; 54:12; 60:3 (= pl. 156:17); 138:13; 156:18; and of 'drill sockets': Guy 1938: pls. 85:15; 135: obj. 612; 153:10.

3. On kilns in general, see H. Hodges 1964:35-39; Scott 1965:391-97; Rhodes 1968:3-17; Holthoer 1977:34-37; Rye 1981:98-110.

4. Since wood is the best fuel for kilns (Rye 1981:104), the pottery industry may have significantly contributed to the deforestation of ancient Palestine.

stacked vessels and out the exit flue. Heat is transferred directly to the vessels by convection and indirectly by radiation after the surfaces of the walls of the kiln become red hot (Rhodes 1968:13, 15).

The Vertical Kiln

The vertical kiln reached its definitive design form in the Early Bronze Age and has remained more or less unchanged to the present day. In this design, the vessels to be fired are placed in a chamber above a fire box, the two being separated by a partition floor supported by a central wall or pillar (fig. 6). A fire is built in the entrance to the fire box. Hot gases then rise through flue holes in the partition floor, pass through the stack of vessels in the upper chamber and out the vent at the top. Thus the designation 'up-draft' kiln. Another feature sometimes found in the vertical kiln is flues in the side walls of the fire box to aid in the convection of heat to the pottery chamber.

Temperatures in the kiln are controlled by the intensity of the fire and the amount of draft. The draft can be regulated by adjusting the size of the air inlet opening, the size of the flue holes in the partition floor (before firing) and the size of the exit flue.

Archaeological Evidence.[1] The best-preserved Syro-Palestinian kiln so far published is Kiln G in Sounding X at Sarepta (Ras al-Qantara, biblical Zarephath) dating to the LB II period (fig. 7.2; Pritchard 1975:72-73; 1978:117-23).[2] It is typical of the vertical kilns used in Palestine and consisted of an almost complete fire chamber, a partition floor with flues, and a doorway leading to an adjoining stoking room. Nothing remained

1. Delcroix and Huot (1972) have collected examples of vertical kilns from various regions of the Near East. The Egyptian evidence, not included in the study of Delcroix and Huot, is surveyed by Holthoer (1977:34-37). For the development of the vertical kiln in Iran, see Alezadeh 1985. Delcroix and Huot divide the vertical kiln into a number of types (II-VI), depending on the exact placement of the various elements, and distinguish it from the simple kiln (their Type I) in which the vessels and fuel are placed together in the same chamber (1972:95).
2. A complete kiln from the New Kingdom period was recently found by Eliezer Oren in the north Sinai (Oren 1987: 99-103).

of the upper chamber where the vessels were stacked for firing. The circular fire chamber was subterranean, which minimized heat losses and provided easy access to the upper chamber from the working surface where the vessels were fabricated. It was formed by lining a pit dug into the debris of earlier occupation with field stones to form a U-shaped wall. Another wall was constructed in the center of the resulting chamber to provide support for the partition floor above. The support wall was 60 cm wide and extended from the back of the U-shaped wall to a point 84 cm from the doorway, allowing for the passage of hot gases to the sides of the chamber. Several layers of clay were applied to the surface of the curved wall as well as to the support wall to form a coating 12–16 cm thick. The fire chamber measured 2.40 m long and 1.85 m wide. The measurement from the floor of the fire chamber to the bottom of the partition floor above was 1.30–1.36 m.

The slightly arched partition floor was composed of several layers of clay with a total thickness of 30–40 cm. Penetrating the partition floor were flues or vents, 33 of which could be identified, 18 being completely preserved (there were probably additional flues in two segments of the floor which had collapsed). Around the outer perimeter was a circle of large flues c. 12 cm in diameter which extended obliquely outward from the fire chamber below. The smaller flues in the central area were vertical. Some of the flues were covered with well-fitting stones, which provided a means of control over the amount of heat passing into the upper pottery chamber. Since there was no evidence of supporting members for the upper chamber of kiln G, Pritchard conjectures that it may have been a temporary structure of clay built around the stacked pottery, with an opening at the top to serve as a chimney and a means of access for closing the large flues around the perimeter of the partition floor (1978:120-21).

The entrance to the lower fire chamber consisted of a passageway c. 1 m long which connected the fire chamber with an adjacent stoking room. Possibly this passageway was roofed over, but no evidence remained. The doorway to the fire chamber had, during the last firing, been almost completely blocked with large stones. This provided a second means of control. By adjusting the size of the doorway, the amount of oxygen passing into the fire chamber and thus the rate of combustion and amount of draft could be controlled.

Another well-preserved vertical kiln was found in the 12th-century Philistine level at Tel Jemmeh (van Beek 1977:172-73; 1983:16; 1984:689-91; Rye 1981: fig. 1). It was egg-shaped in plan, measuring 3.9 × 2.4 m. The wall of the fire chamber was constructed of clay, with retaining walls on the outside. A series of four mud-brick arches anchored in the retaining walls supported the partition floor. The arches were constructed in Egyptian style, with the bricks laid on edge at right angles to the line of the arch, with sherds inserted between the bricks to form the curve of the arch. In the partition floor above, between the arches, were two rows of holes for the passage of heat from the fire chamber to the pottery chamber. A flue was built between each of the arches in the walls of the fire chamber. The passage of each flue sloped upward and was divided into two square-section flues (cf. Bliss 1894:45; Badè 1928:28, pl. XII). Such flues acted to distribute the heat more evenly in the pottery chamber.[1]

1. Other examples of vertical kilns, in addition to those shown in fig. 7, are (a) Chalcolithic–EB I period—Lachish, a double kiln with common draft (Tufnell *et al.* 1958:263). (b) MB I period— 'Afula, three kilns (M. Dothan 1975:34); Har Yeruham, one kiln (Kochavi 1963, 1978; Cohen 1974:133); Khalit el-Fûl, a nearly perfectly preserved vertical (?) kiln (Dever 1969:575-76). (c) MB II period—Jericho, one kiln (Kenyon 1981:364, pls. 193b, 334); Jerishe/Gerisa, one large kiln (Kaplan 1972:76-77; Geva 1982:10, figs. 3, 9, 10, pls. 11:1, 2); Joppa, two kilns; Tel Aviv, two kilns; Tell er-Ridan, one well-preserved kiln (Biran 1974:142); Tell el-Ajjul, two kilns (Petrie 1931:6, pls. 6:2, 3; 54:DF, DK). (d) Middle Bronze or Late Bronze Age—Tell el-Hesi, one kiln with flues in the side walls (Bliss 1894:46-48). (e) Late Bronze Age—Acco, Area A–B, one kiln (M. Dothan and Conrad 1979:227); Acco, Area K, several kilns (M. Dothan and Conrad 1983:114); Deir el-Balah, three kilns (T. Dothan 1981:129); Hazor, Area H, one kiln at the entrance to the Orthostat Temple (Yadin 1972:82, fig. 19; Yadin *et al.* 1989: 230, pl. 38 locus 2160); Sarepta, Sounding X, 21 kilns (Pritchard 1975:71-84; 1978:111-26); Sarepta, Sounding Y, one kiln (Anderson 1975:45-47; 1979:83-85; Pritchard 1978:81). (f) Late Bronze and Iron Ages— Megiddo, East Slope, 11 kilns (Guy 1938:23, 74-82, 102-103, 109, pl. 1: Area R16; cf. Fisher 1929:49-50). (g) Iron I period—'Afula, one kiln (M. Dothan 1975:35); Arad, three kilns (Aharoni 1968:389-91); Ashdod, Area G, one kiln (M. Dothan 1979:129); Ashdod, Area M, four kilns (M. Dothan and Porath 1982:7-8); Tel Miqne, several square kilns (T.

Ethnographic Evidence. Kilns used by village potters in the Middle East today are much like those used in the Bronze and Iron Ages. In Kerami, Jordan, Franken observed a vertical kiln in operation (1969:94-95). The kiln was constructed in a pit, with the top rising only slightly above the surrounding surface. In front of the kiln was a deep hole partially filled with a variety of fuels. The pottery chamber was filled from above by a boy who stood on the unfired pots. It was eventually closed with broken pots and earth when the required temperatures had been reached. Stoking was done by a specialist who constantly watched the color of the fire in the fire chamber and continually fed the fire with small quantities of fuel on which he was sitting.

Matson gives a detailed description of a similar kiln in Vounaria, Greece (1972:217-18). Constructed of sun-dried clay bricks, it was cylindrical in shape with an inside diameter of c. 3.5 m. The fire chamber, located below ground level, was c. 1.0 m high and had a central pillar to support the pottery chamber above. The pottery chamber was c. 1.5 m high with a loading door at the level of the floor and a vent at the top. If kept in repair, the kilns of Vounaria remained in service for two or three generations.

Xanthoudides explains how the itinerant potters of Crete constructed their kilns (1927:126-27). The use of stone arches by the Cretan potters to support the pottery chamber is much like that used in the Philistine kiln at Tel Jemmeh described above.[1]

The Horizontal Kiln

The horizontal kiln represents a more sophisticated design than the simple up-draft kiln. Its design differs from the verti-

Dothan 1989:4-5). (h) Iron II period—Acco, Area A–B, one kiln (M. Dothan and Conrad 1978:265); Acco, Area K, one kiln (M. Dothan and Conrad 1984:190); 'Afula, one kiln (M. Dothan 1975:35); Arad, several kilns near the entrance to the Str. VIII–VII temple (Aharoni 1967:271; 1968:21); Tell en-Nasbeh, one kiln (Badè 1928:28-29, pl. XII; McCown 1947:211, 258, fig. 52B).

1. Additional descriptions of traditional kilns are those of Blackman (1927:148) and Coulson and Wilkie (1986:69, fig. 14) for Egypt; Hampe and Winter (1962: *passim*) for the Aegean; and Köpke (1985) for Spain.

cal kiln in that the elements are arranged along a horizontal rather than a vertical axis (fig. 9). A fire box is located at the front and an exit flue at the back. In between, the vessels are stacked in a chamber for firing. A baffle, or row of pots, is placed at the back of the fire box so as to direct the hot gases to the top of the pottery chamber. The gases are then drawn down through the stack of pots and out the exit flue, leading to the designation 'downdraft' kiln (Scott 1965:382, 393; Rye 1981:100).

A major shortcoming of the vertical kiln is that it is difficult to maintain a constant temperature throughout the pottery chamber. As a result, there is often uneven firing of the wares. This difficulty is overcome in the horizontal kiln by a gradual reduction in cross section in going from the front of the kiln to the back. This is accomplished by making the height or width of the pottery chamber, or both, increasingly smaller. Thus, as the gases cool as heat is transferred to the vessels, the velocity of the gases increases. This results in a more even amount of heat being transferred to all vessels in the chamber, regardless of location (Rhodes 1968:20). As with the vertical kiln, the draft in the horizontal kiln can be controlled by adjusting the sizes of the air inlet opening and the exit flue.

Archaeological Evidence. Horizontal kilns have been found at Deir el-Balaḥ, Tell Jemmeh, Beth Shemesh, and Ashdod. The earliest of these was found in Str. 4 at Deir el-Balaḥ dating to the end of the Late Bronze Age (T. Dothan 1981:127, 129). It was approximately 2.5 × 1.0 m and had a 'bottle-like shape' (1981:129). Details are not yet available on the Tell Jemmeh kiln, mentioned only briefly by T. Dothan (*ibid.*). At Beth Shemesh, one horizontal kiln comes from Str. IVb, dating to the Iron IA period (Wood 1985:453), and another from Str. III, which can be dated to the Iron IB period (Wood 1985:454). Both kilns, identified as metal-working furnaces by the excavator,[1] were very much alike (figs. 10.2, 3). The Str. IVb kiln was c. 4.4 × 0.9 m and was constructed of one course of stones with a clay lining. Fired bricks found in the ruins may have

---

1. Muhly earlier pointed out that the Beth Shemesh 'furnaces' were in fact pottery kilns (1982:53).

come from the superstructure (Grant 1934:20, 42, pls. XII.1, XIII; Grant and Wright 1939:39, pl. VII.2). The Str. III kiln, also constructed of field stones, was c. 2.9 × 0.8 m and slightly wider in the front than in the back. So as to facilitate temperature equalization throughout the kiln, the floors of both kilns were lower in the front than in the back (Grant 1934:52; Grant and Wright 1939:56, pl. IX.3).

In Area D at Ashdod seven kilns, all of the horizontal type, were found in Str. 3 (c. 8th century BCE). The mud brick walls of the lower part of each kiln were built in a pit (fig. 10.1). A shallow hole was dug in front of the mouth of the kiln to serve as a stoking hole, and a brick arch formed the entrance to the kiln. The fire was built in the front and the hot gases from the fire were drawn through the kiln and out an exit flue at the back. No evidence for an exit flue was noted by the excavator, however (M. Dothan 1971:92). Published plans of three of these kilns (1971: pl. 12) indicate that the floor sloped upwards toward the rear, as is typical of horizontal kilns.

Ethnographic Evidence. The horizontal kiln is most common in the East. Foster describes one in Bamunmara, Bengal (1956:396-97). It was a permanent structure of mud brick, triangular in cross section and measuring 3.1 m in length and 2.1 m in width at the base of the triangle. A pit at the apex, separated from the pottery chamber by a grate of pots, served as the fire box. The floor of the pottery chamber inclined upward away from the grate. Three half-pots at floor level in the far wall of the chamber served as exit flues. To fire, the kiln was loaded to a point well above the wall, covered with sherds, and then sealed with a coating of straw and mud. Firing normally began shortly after dusk and continued until about 4 a.m. The intensity of the fire, moderate at first, was stepped up for the final two hours. A small opening was then made in the mud and sherd covering and a pot removed. The condition of the pot told the potter whether the firing was completed or whether more time was necessary. Estimates of the progress of the firing were also made by looking through the exit flues between stokings.

Hankey describes a large horizontal kiln at Beit Shebab, Lebanon (1968:30, 31), as does Rhodes for Ching-te-chen, China (1968:20).

Matson has observed Middle Eastern potters using almost every conceivable type of flammable material as fuel for their kilns. He lists straw, dung cakes, grape vine cuttings, maize stalks and other agricultural wastes, industrial wastes, sawdust, charcoal, oil, old tires, grasses and weeds, wood logs and branches, desert brush, and dried cattails and similar reeds as some of the more important fuels in use today (1966:152; cf. Rice 1987:174-76).

Pottery Workshops

Ancient, as well as modern, ceramicists usually set up their ateliers on the outskirts of town. There are several reasons for this: to be closer to raw materials and fuel, to remove a potential fire hazard and to avoid antagonizing nearby residents with smoke from the kilns (Mendelsohn 1940:17; de Vaux 1965:76; Johnston 1974a:104; Holthoer 1977:27; Rye 1981:9; M. Dothan and Porath 1982:7; Peacock 1982:38; Wright 1985:312, 313). Exceptions to this seem to have been individual shops associated with temples where votive vessels were produced for use by devotees of the cult.

Requirements for a pottery workshop are relatively simple: storage space for raw materials, a basin or floor for preparing the clay, a levigation tank if fine wares are being produced, a potter's wheel, a drying area for newly formed pots and a kiln (Peacock 1982:30; Wright 1985:314; Kramer 1985:80). Apart from the technical requirements of the potter's wheel and the kiln, the most crucial aspect of the workshop layout is the drying facility. While a freshly turned pot is drying to a 'leather-hard' condition, it must be free from strong drafts and direct sunlight, so that all parts of the pot dry at the same rate and thus avoid cracking. A drying shed or cave is therefore imperative much of the time, particularly during excessively damp or hot seasons (Tufnell *et al.* 1958:91; Scott 1965:381; Franken 1969:93; Peacock 1982:39).

Ceramic industries have been studied in contemporary cultures in various parts of the world.These data have been systematized so that we can speak of various pottery production 'models' or 'modes'. Van der Leeuw has discerned six different models: household production, household industry, individual industry, workshop industry, village industry, and large-scale industry (1977; cf. Peacock 1981; 1982:8-50; Arnold 1985:225-31; Rice 1987:176-91). The latter category, so far as is known, does not occur until the Roman period and therefore need not concern us here.

From the foregoing archaeological evidence it is clear that pottery was being produced on a large commercial scale in the Bronze and Iron Ages in Palestine. In order to achieve the quantity and quality of production demanded by this industry, the potter's wheel and permanent kiln were, as our data have attested, necessary items of equipment (Peacock 1982:25). These considerations (mass production, use of a potter's wheel and use of a permanent kiln) point to one or both of two models: the workshop industry and/or the village industry, more appropriately termed the urban industry model in Palestine.

Workshop Industry Production
The workshop industry mode of production is characterized by an individual shop where potting provides the major income for the operators. A master potter mass-produces his wares on a wheel and fires them in a permanent kiln. Several assistants, usually family members, are involved in the process. The workshop industry presumably would have been the predominant mode of production during times of a decentralized economy in the Bronze and Iron Ages, for instance, during the EB IV–MB I period. The individual workshop was also the locus for specialized production, such as producing pottery for a cultic installation.

Archaeological Evidence. A number of well-preserved individual pottery workshops have been excavated in Palestine. The two best-published examples are a LB IIA shop at Hazor and an early Iron I shop at Lachish.[1]

---

1. Other individual workshops are: (a) MB I—Kh. el-Kerak, in the southeast part of the site (Hestrin 1975:256); Har Yeruham, a shop and nearby a kiln with a complete vessel inside and an abundance of pot-

In the lower city of Hazor, in Area C just below the upper city and just inside the southwest rampart, a cultic shrine and associated buildings were found. Part of this complex was a potters' workshop area (fig. 12). It appears to have been two separate workshops once joined by a doorway which was later blocked. The northernmost unit, Building 6225, was only partially excavated. The most significant find here was a low bench with a complete potter's wheel thrust bearing assembly on top, apparently an installation for a potter's wheel (see p. 20 above). Next to the bearings was a pottery cult mask and close by was a potter's forming tool (Yadin *et al.* 1960:101-103, pls. 33.2, 182; 1972:35).

In Building 6063, to the south, two upper bearings were found as well as a number of basalt bowls and pestles. One room with a cobbled floor was likely a clay preparation area while another small room with a drain may have been a soaking or levigation tank. Other rooms in the complex were undoubtedly drying rooms and storage facilities (Yadin *et al.* 1958:77, pls. 25.3; 87:23, 25; 1969:98-101, pls. 32, 33.1; Yadin 1972:32-34). Also of interest are three open-fronted booths just east of the pottery workshops, which faced a roadway leading to the Stelae Shrine (fig. 13). The center booth, the largest, contained a large concentration of pottery vessels (bowls, chalices, goblets, juglets and lamps) nested neatly together, the

tery beside it (Kochavi 1963, 1978; Cohen 1974:133). (b) MB IIB—'Afula, a potter's refuse pit containing unfired Tell el-Yahudiyeh sherds (M. Dothan 1975:35). (c) LB—Hazor, Area H, a workshop at the entrance to the Str. 2 (LB IB) Orthostat Temple comprised of a vertical kiln and a long room (Yadin 1972:82, fig. 19; Yadin *et al.* 1989:230, pl. 38); forming tools were found at the entrance to the temple and in the long room (Yadin *et al.* 1961: pl. 269.27, 28) and a potter's jar was found in the kiln (shown here in fig. 5.1); Sarepta, Sounding Y, a fragmentary portion of a potters' work area in Phases F and E (LB IIB); part of a kiln was found as well as walls, a potter's forming tool and ash pits (Anderson 1975:45-47; 1979:81-108; Pritchard 1978:79-82). (d) Iron I— Arad, a workshop with three variously shaped ovens, charred beams and various pottery vessels (Aharoni 1967:270); Lachish, Cave 6034 (Tufnell 1953:250-52) was used by potters as evidenced by potters' forming tools (*ibid.*, pls. 41.12, 58.2, 14) and potters' jars (shown here in figs. 5.6, 7). From the Iron II period is a biblical reference to the 'house of the potter'(*bêt hayyôsēr*) in Jer. 18.2, indicating the workplace of an individual potter.

bottom of a cult stand and a bronze silver-plated standard
bearing a cultic relief. It has been speculated that these booths
were shops where cultic items were sold to devotees of the
shrine (Yadin *et al.* 1960:104-106, pl. 35; Yadin 1972:36-37).

Caves make excellent work areas for pottery production
since they not only afford comfortable working conditions for
the potter, but they also provide a good place to dry freshly-
made vessels. Such a cave-workshop was found at Lachish in
Cave 4034. It was located on the north slope of the tell, in the
4000 Cemetery area, not far from the main source of water.
From the pottery that was left behind, it appears that operations here ceased when Level VI was destroyed in the mid-
12th century BCE (Tufnell *et al.* 1958:293; Ussishkin
1983:170).

Inside the cave were three small pits and a subterranean
chamber with steps leading to the bottom (fig. 14). Heaps of
raw material, including prepared clay, crushed lime and
shells, charcoal, and lumps of red and yellow ochre, were
found on the floor, in Pit A and in the subterranean chamber
(Pit B) (Tufnell *et al.* 1958:91, 292). Pit A, over 2 m deep, evidently served as a dump for the artisans, as it was full of discarded items from their trade. In it were quantities of unbaked
sherds, a fragment of a figurine mold, an incomplete figurine,
broken trial pieces and vessels, and various potters' tools.
Among the potters' tools were two upper thrust bearings (figs.
2.1, 2), forming tools (Tufnell *et al.* 1958: pl. 49.15), burnishing
tools (polished pebbles and shells), a bone point, a small limestone mortar used for grinding red ochre (1958: pl. 49.14) and
four potters' jars (figs. 5.3-5) (1958:91, 196, 292). The sunken
chamber, Pit B, evidently served as a drying room and storage
area. At the bottom of the steps was a stone mortar c. 50 cm in
diameter and on the floor were finished bowls of various kinds
(1958:91, 292, 293). Pits C and D appear to be emplacements
for potters' wheels (see pp. 21-22 above).

Ethnographic Evidence. The organization and day-to-day
operation of workshops by families and small groups involved
in the commercial production of pottery in contemporary
peasant societies cannot have differed significantly from that
of ancient Palestine. In most peasant cultures, pottery making

is an economic adaptation brought about by population pressure (Arnold 1985:168-201). A region which has poor agricultural land often will have the necessary raw materials for ceramic production. In an area where weathering and erosion have removed the nutrient-rich topsoil and destroyed land by stream cutting, the same forces have frequently exposed excellent ceramic resources. In such an agriculturally marginal area, the residents are forced to turn to additional means of livelihood to supplement their meagre crops; since ceramic raw materials are often readily available, pottery production becomes one of these supplementary means of income (Arnold 1978:46, 51-52; Reina and Hill 1978:xx, 17; Nicklin 1979:453-54; Kramer 1985:80). The availability of suitable raw materials may, in turn, lead to specialized villages, which supply pottery to those in other areas who do not need to, do not wish to, or cannot make their own pottery (Foster 1965:45; Reina and Hill 1978:xx, 17). In Palestine, however, raw materials are readily available in nearly all parts of the country, conforming well to the archaeological observation that ceramic production was widely practiced in antiquity (see p. 49 below). In addition, it is probable that in ancient Palestine, as elsewhere, those who did not have access to land were forced into potting or similar trades. Most contemporary village potters would rather be full-time farmers but, for one reason or another, are not able to do so (Arnold 1985:193).

A pottery workshop in modern-day Palestine has been described by M. Dothan (1971:90-92). It consisted of a courtyard containing two kilns and a basin for preparing the clay, and a number of adjacent rooms for turning, drying, and storing the vessels (1971:91). The shop was operated by two male potters who produced six types of vessels, each type being produced in two or three sizes (store jars, plates, drums, children's saving boxes, jugs, and bowls).

Xanthoudides observed a group of potters from Thrapsanos, Crete, who fabricated vessels very similar to those of antiquity (1927:120). One group or workshop of Cretan potters consisted of from seven to twelve men, each specializing in one or more tasks. The master potter directed the operations of the group and made pithoi on a hand-turned wheel; a second potter made all of the other vessels on a foot-operated double wheel. Other specialists included a boy apprentice, who turned the wheel for the master potter, a kiln stoker, a man who dug the clay, a man who cut wood for fuel, and a man who brought the clay and wood to the work area. Although each man had a particular speciality, some tasks were shared, such as the kneading of the clay and transporting the finished wares to the place where they were to be sold (1927:127-28; cf. Voyatzoglou 1974:18).[1]

After observing many contemporary village potters in the Middle East, Matson has noted the seasonal nature of their work. They concentrate their productive efforts in the spring and summer months when the weather is suitable for drying the wares and keeping the fuel and kilns dry. In many areas the potters farm their own lands, thus requiring them to integrate their potting with the agricultural cycles (1966:151). In Beit Shebab, Lebanon, the potting season is from May to late September (Hankey 1968:28).

Pottery making is a low-status position in most societies. Potters have a low opinion of themselves and would rather be doing something else for their livelihood. Most are forced to continue in the trade, however, because of limited opportunities in other occupations. Pottery making is considered 'dirty work' and potters are generally looked down upon by non-potters (Foster 1965:46-47; Nicholson and Paterson 1985a:59; 1985b:236; Arnold 1985:196-98; Rice 1987:172).[2]

Urban Industry Production
By reason of the availability of raw materials, fuel, demand, and market opportunities, a large number of potteries will many times cluster in one locale, resulting in what van der

1. Two workshops in Egypt are described by Nicholson and Patterson (1985a:55-57; 1985b:229-30) and Coulson and Wilkie (1986:68, fig. 13). For additional ethnographic examples of individual ceramic workshops in Europe and the Mediterranean area, see Peacock 1982:31-48.

2. David and Hennig note that in Bé in North Cameroon, 'the hallmark of the successful potter is to have stopped potting' (1972:25). Pottery making by women in the Rif mountains of Morocco is considered 'socially despicable' work (Vossen 1984:374). In the Sudan, potters and blacksmiths are stigmatized statuses (Haaland 1978:57), as is the case in Ethiopia (Matson 1965:212).

Leeuw calls the 'village industry' mode of production. The individual shop is basically the same as that in the workshop industry mode, but now there are many shops exploiting the same raw materials, fuel and markets. During periods of intense urbanization, i.e. during the EB II–III, MB II, Late Bronze and Iron Age periods, the village industry mode would probably have been the dominant mode of production.[1] In Palestine, this mode of production is more appropriately termed the 'urban industry' mode since it would appear that the ceramic industry was concentrated in the urban centers.

The urban industry mode of production is characterized by a high-volume output of a fairly standardized range of good-quality products. It can be subdivided into two types: discrete workshops and nucleated workshops. With discrete workshops, the potters maintain their workplaces within the confines of their own homes, although there will be many potters grouped together in one locale. In the nucleated mode, the workshops are separate from the potters' homes and are clustered together to form a tightly-knit industrial complex.

There are a number of benefits to be gained by establishing many workshops in one area. One is the development of ancillary services. These take the form of raw material supply, fuel supply, transport, kiln building and the like. In contemporary examples, cooperation between shops seems to be the rule rather than the exception. Mutual aid, especially in times of

1. There are, of course, exceptions to this broad generalization. It is possible for different modes of ceramic production to exist side-by-side in a given society (Arnold 1985:237). In the EB III period, for example, refiring experiments indicate that Khirbet Kerak ware was fired in open bonfires (Chazan and McGovern 1984). This would suggest that Khirbet Kerak ware was made according to van der Leeuw's 'household industry' mode of production. In the LB IIB and Iron I periods, crude hand-made 'Negev' pottery appears alongside commercially produced wares in the southern part of the country (Sheffer 1976). This was no doubt a product of the 'household production' mode.

misfortune, is commonplace and capital expenditures are
many times shared through cooperative schemes (Peacock
1982:9, 43).

Archaeological Evidence. Although we lack good examples of
urban industry production with discrete workshops,[1] we have
three excellent examples of nucleated pottery production. The
earliest of these is at Sarepta on the Lebanese coast.

A 20 × 30 m area on the gentle western slope of Sarepta was
found to have been entirely devoted to the ceramic industry
(Pritchard 1975:71-84; 1978:111-26). Pottery making was
carried on here for about a millennium during the Late
Bronze Age and Iron Ages. In this 600 m² area (Sounding X)
the remains of some 22 vertical kilns were found, with as
many as 12 in operation at one time (Pritchard 1978:113). The
quarter was separated into individual work areas by low
divider walls; one such work area was Room 74 from the LB
IIB period (Pritchard 1975: fig. 14 = 1978: fig. 113). It was c. 6.4
× 7.6 m and had a floor of yellow clay c. 3 cm thick. The divider
walls were coated with 6–8 cm. of the same yellow clay. In the
center of the area was a circular depression, with a diameter
of c. 1.50 m and a depth of 15–18 cm. It sloped gently from the
general floor level toward a bottom of stones (Pritchard
1975:74; 1978:120). Scattered about the area were various
remains from the potters' work: piles of finely levigated yellow
clay, basins of various sizes and shapes, a forming tool
(Pritchard 1975: fig. 29.7) and, adjacent to the nearby kilns,
heaps of 'waster' sherds from vessels that had been ruined in
the firing process (Pritchard 1975:19; 1978:111, 113). No potter's wheel thrust bearings were found, but a cemented installation appears to have been the seat for a lower thrust bearing
(Pritchard 1975:72).

The most extensive pottery workshop area yet found in
Palestine is on the east slope of the Megiddo mound.[2] As at

1. Two kilns in close proximity in the lower city of Tell el-Ajjul (MB
IIC period) appear to be associated with domestic units. The data,
however, are insufficient to allow a positive determination to be made
(Petrie 1931:6, pl. 54: DF, DK).

2. For a summary of the evidence, see Wood 1985: fig. 2.3 and table
2.1.

Lachish, the Megiddo ceramicists set up their shops in the
various caves that dot the hillside. This was a cemetery area in
antiquity—a common place to find pottery workshops
(Matson 1974:346). At least 12 kilns were found (e.g. fig. 7.3),
as well as other evidence for the pottery industry such as potter's wheel thrust bearings (figs. 2.6, 8, 9) and forming tools
(Guy 1938: 23 n. 1). A number of the caves had subterranean
chambers, evidently used as drying rooms (Guy 1938: *passim*).
Although it is difficult to date the period of use of the various
potters' caves with certainty, the associated pottery indicates
that they were in use in the Late Bronze and Iron Ages.

In Area D at Ashdod, southwest of the main area of occupation, a number of connected workshops were found (M.
Dothan 1971:89-92). A total of seven horizontal kilns from
three different phases of the Iron II period were excavated, as
well as two vertical kilns from the Hellenistic period. The best
preserved of the Iron Age phases was Str. 3a from the latter
part of the 8th century BCE (M. Dothan and Porath 1982:57 n.
23). Three kilns, Nos. 1088 (fig. 10.1), 1164 and 1168, were
attributed to this phase. They were in a series of walled-in
areas of varying size arranged along a north-south axis (fig.
15). The walls and floors of the kilns were covered with layers
of ash and lumps of slag. Fragments of wasters were found
inside and outside the kilns. Some 35 m north of the kiln complex two additional rooms were excavated (fig. 15.1179, 1180).
Although no kilns were found in these rooms, kiln debris and
quantities of slag indicate that the potters' quarter extended
this far. The unexcavated area between rooms 1174 and 1179
was littered with slag deposits as well.[1]

---

1. In Ashdod Area M, east of the acropolis, fragmentary remains of a
pottery manufacturing area dating to the Iron I period were found.
Portions of four kilns were excavated, as well as refuse pits filled with
ash and kiln rejects, and sections of pebble floors (M. Dothan and
Porath 1982:7-8). In Jer. 19.1 mention is made of the 'Gate of the Pot-
sherds' in Jerusalem which led to the Hinnom Valley on the west and
south sides of the city. Possibly the area outside the 'Gate of the Pot-
sherds' was given over to the production of pottery. In ancient Athens
the potters congregated in one district of the city called the *Ceramicus*
(H.A. Thompson 1984). A potters' quarter has been excavated at
Corinth (Stillwell 1948).

Ethnographic Evidence. We have numerous examples of the
village industry mode of production in contemporary pottery-
producing societies. Both discrete and nucleated types have
been documented, with discrete being the most prevalent.

Along the west shore of the Messenian Gulf in Greece, there
are a number of pottery-producing villages. Raw materials
and fuel are abundant there, as well as ports from which to
distribute the finished products (Matson 1972:213). The pottery shops in these villages are operated by families, with the
sons learning the craft from their fathers; some of them have
'been making pottery for as long as they have any record—a
long, long time' (1972:221).

In Bailén, Spain, pottery making is the only industry in this
small town of c. 13,000 people (in 1973). The workshops are
family operated by the men of the family, with the business
being handed down from father to son, generation after generation. There are between 40 and 70 shops, all located in the
homes of their owners (Vossen 1984:346, 348). The smallest
shop, which produces a little under 100,000 vessels in a season,
has one kiln and two wheels and employs four men. The
largest shop, producing some 300,000 vessels per season, has
three kilns and 12 wheels and employs 20 men. Pottery making is a full-time occupation for the potters of Bailén. During
the rainy season (September–March) when little pottery is
made, preparations are made for the coming potting season:
supplies are purchased, kilns are repaired, clay storage pits
are cleaned and prepared, and contacts for future sales are
made (Curtis 1962:487-88).[1]

Foster has investigated the pottery industry of Tzintzuntzan, Mexico, a town of 1200 people (in 1945) specializing
in the production of utilitarian ceramic wares. Sixty percent of
the people in Tzintzuntzan depend entirely, or in part, on
pottery making for their livelihood. The most common productive unit is the nuclear family in which husband, wife and
children cooperate in the entire process. The men gather clays

1. There are also large village industries in Salvatierra de los Barros,
Spain (c. 50 shops in 1973), and Agost, Spain (c. 20 shops in 1973). See
Llorens Artigas and Corredor-Matheos 1974:95 and Vossen 1984:341-
46, 352-59.

and firewood, while women alone grind the glaze, since this is *metate* work. Both sexes prepare paste, fabricate the pots (using molds), decorate them, participate in firing in a permanent vertical kiln[1] and help with selling. The potters usually specialize in making a particular object, but are familiar with the basic techniques for fabricating any of the products turned out by the unit. They are artisans who turn out work meeting a basic standard and do not make an effort to surpass that standard. No individual marks of manufacture are used. The potters consider their work as simply an occupation to earn a living and few find it interesting. Pottery making in Tzintzuntzan is a hereditary craft, passed down in family lines through either the father's or the mother's side, or both. But since there are no secrets in making the traditional wares, anyone can learn to be a potter (Foster 1965:44-46, 52).

The potters of Tzintzuntzan have a low opinion of themselves and would rather be farmers or storekeepers. Although they participate fully in civic and religious activities, they are looked down upon by non-potters. Pottery making in Tzintzuntzan is considered 'dirty work', but the chances of giving up the trade are slim because of limited agricultural land and the lack of other types of occupations (1965:46-47).[2]

Nucleated ceramic industries such as were operating in the Bronze and Iron Ages in Palestine are still functioning in parts of the Middle East. One is known at Deir el-Gharbi, Egypt, and another at Djerba, Tunisia.

At Deir el-Gharbi, 40 km north of Luxor, an amphora-like jar is produced, called a *Ballas*, named after a nearby village. The dying industry has recently been studied by Nicholson and Patterson (1985a, 1985b). Their findings may be summarized as follows. There are some 15 shops in the village, all located at the edge of the settlement bordering the desert. As little as ten years prior to the study (done in 1984), there were scores of pottery workshops in the area. Each shop is independently owned and is staffed by a potter and three assistants, all

1. Vertical kilns used throughout Mexico and South America are identical in design to those used in ancient Palestine and the Middle East today. See, e.g., Litto 1976:38.
2. Other villages in Peru, Chile, Columbia, and Venezuela which produce traditional pottery are reported by Litto (1976: *passim*).

male. The shops are clustered in groups of three to five around their respective clay puddling pits and wells, with the kilns lying off to one side. Two shops often share a common wall, with a window linking the two units.

Clay is mined in the nearby hills of the western desert. The miners are a separate profession from that of the potters. Each group of miners supplies specific potters, but does not belong to any particular workshop, nor to the same family as the potters. The miners are considered to be of a lower status than the potters. Blocks of clay are loaded on donkeys or camels for the short 45 minute walk to the workshop area.

Once at the workshop, the blocks of clay are broken into smaller lumps and placed in stone-lined soaking pits for softening. The pits are c. 50 cm deep and 2.5–3.0 m in diameter and are connected by channels to a well. It is not unusual for one well to be shared by two workshops. A spirit of cooperation exists between shops and there is considerable sharing of facilities. After soaking overnight, the clay is first trampled by two water buffalo hired from nearby agriculturalists. It is then taken inside the shop where it is further trampled on a cobbled floor by two of the potter's assistants.

Work in the Deir el-Gharbi potters' quarter begins at 5 a.m. and continues to 5 p.m. While his assistants perform a variety of supporting tasks, the potter spends the entire day at his wheel. The double wheel is located on one side of a room, c. 5 × 6 m, with a cobbled floor (the same room where the clay is trampled). As was the case in the potters' caves at Lachish and Megiddo, the flywheel is located in a shallow pit in the floor. Adjacent to the work room is a long narrow drying room, c. 4 × 12 m.

The jars are fired in large vertical kilns c. 5 m in diameter which hold 500–700 vessels. Each vessel is stacked inverted, separated from the one below by a sherd. The kiln is densely packed to the top of the wall. A covering of sherds is then placed over the vessels. Sorghum stems purchased from the agriculturalists are used for fuel. Firing begins at 5 a.m. and continues for three and a half to four hours, after which the kiln is allowed to cool for two days. Between five and ten percent of the vessels in each firing are wasters.

On the island of Djerba, off the coast of southern Tunisia, a major pottery center is in operation at Guellala on the south side of the island (Combès and Louis 1967; Peacock 1982:41-42; Johnston 1984). In 1967 there were 157 workshops spread over an area of c. 31 km.[2] Although a range of forms is produced, the main stock-in-trade is a large amphora-like jar. In order to protect themselves and their products from the heat, the potters have constructed underground workshops. Clay is softened in small tanks 2–4 m long and 1–1.5 m wide. Double wheels are used which employ a wooden shaft turning in a stone socket embedded in the workshop floor. Firing, which takes about three days, is done in both large and small vertical kilns using wood and palm fronds as fuel. About 160 large oil jars can be fired in one kiln load.

Potters' Marks

The enigmatic marks found on ancient sherds and pots in Palestine have long been associated with a professional pottery industry.[1] There is lack of agreement, however, as to their precise function. In 1940 Mendelsohn suggested that the marks are trade marks, each design belonging to a particular guild of potters (21; cf. Saller 1964:72; de Vaux 1965:77). Forshey has recently examined the Halif materials and concludes, 'it seems unlikely that a single function can be found to explain all of the potter's (*sic*) marks which are known' (1983:2). He went on to suggest tentatively that marks on Late Bronze Age store jar handles at Halif may be an indication of the contents of the vessels (*ibid.*). The excavators of Ashdod believe that an eighth-century incised inscription ([ ] *phr*) may be part of a potter's name written in Aramaic, i.e. '[N the] potter' (M. Dothan and Freedman 1967:84-85). A provenience study of marked Iron Age cooking pots from Yokne'am and Qiri suggests that they were all made from the same clay source and thus possibly from the same workshop (Sharon, Yellin, and Perlman 1987).

---

1. We are considering here incised marks and not stamps, which represent a separate category. On potters' marks in the Aegean, see Frankel 1975 and Bikaki 1984.

Archaeological Evidence
Although these marks have yet to be systematically studied, a few preliminary observations can be made:

1. The marks are placed on the vessels during the fabrication process, i.e. before firing.[1]
2. Only a small percentage of vessels have the marks (Forshey 1984).
3. Similar marks are found at numerous sites from EB I through Iron II (Forshey 1983:1; for an example see Yadin 1974:34 and 1976:6).
4. The marks are found on all types of vessels (Forshey 1984).
5. The same mark is found on contemporary jars of significantly different size. This would tend to rule out the possibility that the marks indicate vessel capacity (Forshey 1983:2).
6. Some of the marks seem to be alphabetic signs (Cross 1954:24; Saller 1964:72-73; Seger 1983).

Ethnographic Evidence
While conducting a surface survey on the north coast of Peru, Donnan noted that about ten percent of plain-ware vessels of the Moche style, a type of pottery which flourished from c. 100 BCE to 800 CE, had marks which were incised prior to firing (1971:461). He also noted that contemporary vessels in central Peru have similar markings. Upon investigating the contemporary marks, Donnan learned that they were applied in order to differentiate the vessels of one potter from those of another during the manufacturing process. The potters utilize these marks when working in their home workshops and also when doing itinerant potting.

One of the most important pottery-making communities in central Peru is Taricá. Here, all aspects of ceramic production, from quarrying the clay to marketing the finished product, are generally carried out by the members of a single family, all of whom comprise a single economic unit. In some cases, how-

1. Markings are incised on vessels after firing as well, but here we are considering only those placed on vessels before firing.

ever, not all of the people involved in producing a given lot of pots are part of a' single economic unit. This can arise from a number of circumstances: a potter from outside the family working on a per unit basis, two or more families sharing the same working area or drying facility, or two different families firing their pots together to conserve fuel. In these instances, one or more of the parties involved will incise a distinctive mark on his pots. This serves to distinguish the pots produced by each of the various parties until the pots are marketed (1971: 465).

The second instance in which the marks are used is in itinerant potting. In central Peru, itinerant potters carry clay to distant isolated communities where there is no local source of good clay. Once they reach a community, they go from house to house taking orders. The requested pots are then made on the spot. Usually, all the potters belong to a single family or economic unit, in which case none of the pots are incised. At times, however, several independent potters representing distinct economic units will travel together. In this case, although each potter makes his pots separately, the pots of two or more potters are usually fired together in order to save fuel. When the pots are fired communally, each potter puts his own distinctive mark on his pots so that they can be easily identified when they are retrieved from the ashes after firing (1971; cf. Donnan 1973:94-95).

The potters of Taricá refer to the incised mark as a *signal*. This word is not found in the Spanish dictionary, but Donnan believes that it may be derived from the word *signar*, a transitive verb meaning to sign or mark with a seal (1971:465). The marks have no particular significance to the potters. Donnan notes that the potters often change their *signal* so that the marks cannot be used to identify the work of a given potter. 'The function of the incised marks seems to be simply to prevent confusing the pots of one potter with those of another during manufacturing, and prior to marketing' (*ibid.*).[1]

In future work on potters' marks, I suggest that the above explanation be adopted as a working hypothesis to explain the

---

1. Potts reached a similar conclusion concerning the potters' marks from Tepe Yahya, Iran (1981:108 n. 3; cf. Rice 1987:183).

function of potters' marks in ancient Palestine, to be tested by
further research and analysis.

Potters' Guilds

Literary Evidence

From the archaeological evidence at hand, it appears that
Bronze and Iron Age potters worked in small shops and that
these shops were clustered together in the various urban centers of the region. This accords well with the view of Mendelsohn (1940) that the potters of ancient Palestine were organized into guilds. The individual shops were no doubt run by
families who continued the tradition from generation to generation (de Vaux 1965:77; Heltzer 1982:100).

The literary evidence from Ugarit suggests that some of
these guilds were under the control of the centralized bureaucracy (Rainey 1962:28; Heltzer 1969:38-39). In the 13th century BCE, the city-states of Palestine were declining in power
and probably by the end of the century all of the guilds were
independent (Zaccagnini 1983:258). Some of the potters were
in the employ of, or worked in close coordination with, religious institutions as well. This is evidenced by workshops at or
near cultic centers, as at the Hazor Stelae Shrine (fig. 13), the
Hazor Orthostat Temple (p. 35 n. 1), and at Arad (p. 29 n. 1).

The economic and administrative texts from Ugarit provide
a wealth of information on the status of artisans attached to a
city-state bureaucracy in the 14th–13th centuries BCE.
Heltzer has assembled the pertinent data (1965). The texts
reveal that artisans who were in royal service were provided
the raw materials necessary for their craft. They were paid
wages in silver and in kind from the royal stores and they also
received land in service tenureship. Each craft was organized
with its own 'elders'. The administration often dealt with the
group as a whole, requiring military and other services not
directly related to the profession of its members. The artisans
were royal dependants, but not slaves, and enjoyed the same
social, economic and juridical status as other groups in royal
service such as administrators, military professionals and
priests (Heltzer 1965:59-60; cf. 1982:80-102). Some of the

king's potters were assigned to work at royal estates located in rural areas (Heltzer 1982:74).[1]

Ethnographic Evidence
Potters in peasant societies who are part-time or full-time specialists producing for a commercial market usually form recognized groups such as craft villages, classes or castes (as in India) (Foster 1965:55; Casson 1938:467). The potters of Royerbazar, Bengal, for example, are members of a highly organized trade guild (Foster 1956:404). In north and west Africa, potters' guilds are common (Balfet 1965:163; Nicklin 1971:13) and in west Tibet the itinerant potters are organized into a guild (Asboe 1946:10).

Summary and Conclusions

Nature of the Ceramic Industry
From the archaeological and ethnographic evidence, several conclusions can be drawn concerning pottery production in Bronze and Iron Age Palestine. These conclusions, it must be pointed out, apply to urban centers, since that is largely where excavations have been undertaken and where evidence for pottery production has been found. It is apparent that in the urban centers pottery was mass-produced on a commercial basis. This production was carried out by men in small family workshops that may have been organized into guilds. The technological level was high, with both single and double wheels being used to form the vessels and permanent vertical or horizontal kilns being used to fire them. During non-urbanized periods, production was along the lines of van der Leeuw's 'workshop industry' model. In the urbanized periods, production reached the highest level of industrial production known in the pre-Roman era, the 'village industry' mode of production.

---

1. According to 1 Chron. 4.23, the potters who lived at Nataim and Gederah were in royal service. Demsky has argued that Achzib was a royal pottery production center in the Iron II period (1966:215).

Distribution of the Ceramic Industry

From the location of the potters' workshops, kilns, potter's wheel thrust bearings, and other potters' tools (fig. 16), we can conclude that the ceramic industry was widespread in ancient Palestine. There is no shortage of good clay in Palestine (Johnston 1974a:88; Bender 1974:168), so that pottery could be produced in nearly any location where there was a sufficient market to make it profitable.

PART II

THE DIFFUSION OF CERAMIC STYLE

Ethnoarchaeological research in pottery-making societies has produced a number of cautionary tales. In clarifying many aspects of the productive process, as well as a range of circumstances in which vessels are acquired, used and abused, and discarded, it has also quashed some simplifying notions, illuminated a range of behavioral diversity, and begun to outline model patterns of considerable potential value to archaeologists (Kramer 1985:97).

The use of pottery for studies in chronology, cultural affinities and trade contacts is basic to Palestinian archaeology. Flinders Petrie was the first to recognize the value of pottery for chronological purposes in his historic work at Tell el-Hesi in 1890. He observed that pottery styles[1] gradually change through time, so that once the dates of the various styles are established, the pottery itself can be used as a reliable chronological indicator (1891:1).[2] His method of separating the pottery according to the stratigraphic levels of the tell has been fundamental to Palestinian archaeology ever since.

---

1. Style can refer to both the morphological characteristics of a vessel and its decoration. In this study we are mainly concerned with morphological features.

2. Petrie and his colleague J. Garrow Duncan compiled a corpus of Palestinian pottery in 1930 (Duncan). Additional material from Tell el-Far'ah (S) was later incorporated (Starkey and Harding 1932: pls. 84-88). It was not until Albright published the results of his excavation at Tell Beit Mirsim conducted in the 1920s, however, that Palestinian ceramic chronology was put on a firm scientific basis (Albright 1932, 1933, 1938, 1943). The basic ceramic catalogue used by Palestinian archaeologists today, although badly in need of updating, is Amiran's *Ancient Pottery of the Holy Land* (1969). For further discussion, see Borowski 1988.

Coupled with this gradual change in pottery style at a given site is the fact that, at least from the EB I period onward, pottery with similar morphological attributes is found in widely separated areas (Balfet 1965:175-76; Esse 1982:327; Gerstenblith 1983:84). Thus, if a vessel with chronologically diagnostic features can be dated at one site, parallel vessels are similarly dated at other sites. This method of comparative analysis has been the cornerstone of Palestinian archaeology from its earliest beginnings. Kathleen Kenyon succinctly stated this principle as follows:

> Moreover, conservation and imitativeness as human characteristics have resulted in the widespread use of similar forms of vessels among allied peoples, and of the almost contemporary spread of newly introduced types. We can therefore say that groups of people in, say Early Bronze Age Palestine, using the same type of pottery, are approximately contemporary (1979:15; cf. Franken 1971:228, 253).

But are we justified in making such an assumption? What does Kenyon mean by 'approximately contemporary'—within one year, one decade, one generation? What was the mechanism for the diffusion of pottery style? Until we understand this mechanism, it is not possible adequately to define 'approximately contemporary'.

Franken questions this basic premise and believes that 'the development of a small village like Deir 'Allā may have been well behind that of a settlement found on the Mediterranean coast' (Franken 1969:176; cf. 246 and 1971:253-54). Most researchers either ignore, or are skeptical about (e.g. Lapp 1970:254), the question Franken raises as to the possibility of time lag in the diffusion of ceramic style.

Deetz and Dethlefsen contend that a ceramic type originates at a single locus and spreads outward from that point (1965:196). Such a diffusion through space, of course, will take a finite amount of time. In order to check the theoretical model which predicts the effects of such diffusion, Deetz and Dethlefsen used data from their study of the spread of colonial gravestone designs in New England. These data tend to support the model (1965:205) and suggest that the time lag involved in the diffusion of a particular style from one location to another may be as much as 1 mile per year (Deetz and Dethlefsen 1967:32-33; cf. Dethlefsen and Deetz 1966).

Does the diffusion of 18th and 19th century CE gravestone styles in America have any bearing on pottery styles in ancient Palestine? If the spread of ceramic style in ancient Palestine is anywhere near the 1 mile per year of colonial gravestone styles, then Kenyon's premise 'of the almost contemporary spread of newly introduced types' is seriously called into question and the very foundation of Palestine ceramic chronology and comparative ceramic analysis will have to be reevaluated (McClellan 1975:330-31). In order to answer this challenge, it is first necessary to determine the mode of diffusion of ceramic style in ancient Palestine. This can only be done through an understanding of the total social and economic context in which pottery was manufactured and marketed.

A related problem is that of temporal style variability. If pottery workshops across the land were turning out vessels of similar style, what were the circumstances that caused ceramic style to change through time in a similar fashion at all of these workshops?

A second area of chronometric importance is the matter of vessel lifespan. Even if it can be determined that two similar vessels were manufactured at the same time, if the lifespan of that particular type of vessel is significant, then the two examples may not be contemporary as far as the date of their final use is concerned.

These questions concerning ceramic diffusion and lifespan are of the utmost importance to the archaeologist. They affect the accuracy of ceramic chronology and the validity of comparing the ceramic repertoire of one site to that of another. In this part of the study we shall examine the archaeological, literary and ethnographic evidence in order to formulate an objective judgment concerning these questions rather than depending on subjective opinion, as has been the case in the past. Our discussion will center around three major problems: the spatial diffusion of ceramic style, the temporal variability of ceramic style, and vessel lifespan.

Spatial Diffusion of Ceramic Style

We shall first consider the question of the homogeneity of
Palestinian pottery, i.e. why it is that we find the same style of
pottery in widely separated parts of the country.[1] In Part I of
this study we determined that ceramic wares were produced
in urban centers throughout the region. What were the influences at work at these various centers which caused the potters to produce the same vessel types with nearly identical
morphological attributes?

Ceramic similarity over great distances is commonly
observed by archaeologists and, in fact, is relied upon by them
for chronological links between sites. This same phenomenon
has been noted by ethnographers as well. In the Sudan, Haaland notes that sedentary people in the north use the same
type of pottery as pastoralists 250 km to the south (1978:60). In
North Africa, all of the handmade pottery of the Maghreb
region belongs to the same stylistic and technical family
(Balfet 1965:168). Because of the mobility of the Fulani potters
of North Cameroon, potters become familiar with the ware of
several towns and villages. This has resulted in a similarity of
form and decoration in all of the Fulani pottery in North
Cameroon (David and Hennig 1972:5).

The underlying cause for ceramic similarity in widespread
areas has been given little attention (Davis 1983:54) and the
mechanism for the spread of similar ceramic styles is little
understood.[2] Hodder calls attention to the fact that there is a

---

1. The term 'homogeneity' is used here in a general sense. We are
not implying that contemporary ceramic assemblages are exactly the
same everywhere. What is meant is that vessels with nearly identical
morphological characteristics can be observed in different areas. Certainly there are regional distinctions (see below).
2. Logic dictates that the spread of style will be related to the amount
of interaction between communities. This interaction, however, is a
complex matter and difficult to predict, as illustrated by the example of
Bé cited below. Attempts have been made to express interaction mathematically in the so-called 'Gravity Model': the amount of interaction
between two communities is directly proportional to their population
and inversely proportional to the distance between them (Plog 1976:256;
cf. 1980). Similarly, Rands postulates that 'the archaeologist should
find a sharply reduced amount of the pottery in question as he passed
(*sic*) to sites beyond the border of the sustaining area' (1967:148). Quan-

lack of ethnographic data on the relationship between social structure and cultural diffusion (1978:246).

The problem of the diffusion of ceramic style is an involved one because of the multitude of contributing factors. An illustration of the complexity of the ceramic demography of a peasant community is given by David and Hennig in their study of the pottery of the Fulani village of Bé in North Cameroon.

The Example of Bé
The Fulani seized their present territory in North Cameroon by military conquest in the early part of the 19th century CE. They were mainly pastoralists, although a number of them were involved in the slave trade. As a result of cattle epidemics at the end of the 19th and early in the 20th century and the repression of slave trading, most of the Fulani were forced into subsistence farming. They are organized into chiefdoms; 80 percent of the total population of 300,000 live in small villages and make their living by farming. Some six percent of the Fulani are herders who leave their villages in the dry season to pasture their (and others') cattle in favored areas (David and Hennig 1972:2).

The village of Bé was captured by the Fulani in 1839. Many of its inhabitants were enslaved, while survivors of the siege escaped to the south. Bé in many respects, particularly social organization, resembles a small city-state of Bronze Age Palestine. The village is the capital of a small chiefdom comprising some 6000 people. Six hamlets lie nearby, linked to the village by ties of kinship and by the weekly market and the Friday mosque. The village has 305 residents and a number of laborers which fluctuates seasonally between 10 and 50. The families, nuclear or polygynous, live in fenced compounds of daub huts with conical thatched roofs. There are 243 Fulani and assimilates; the remainder are recent immigrants. All but eight of these immigrants are Gisiga from a region 110 km to the north (1972:3).

titative evaluations, however, regardless of their merits or shortcomings, do not explain the mechanisms involved. For a general discussion of style change, see Hill 1985.

In Fulani society, women own the vast majority of the pots and are responsible for purchasing the pottery for the household. Of a total of 113 adult women in Bé, David and Hennig conducted a census of the pottery in 15 Fulani and 6 Gisiga womens' quarters (a total of 370 pots). They found that 25 percent of the pots were made in the village of Bé itself,[1] 45 percent came from hamlets within a radius of 3 km and 25 percent were purchased at three larger markets within a radius of 22 km, although the pottery may have travelled a similar distance between its place of manufacture and the market. Five percent of the pots in the sample came from distances greater than 22 km. Each Gisiga family, when moving to Bé, brought along one or two pots. There were a number of casual imports brought by women on the occasion of their marriage or by visitors as gifts (1972:4, 14, 16, 17, 22).

The pottery made in the village of Bé is an interesting study in itself. Although David and Hennig did not trace the history of each individual pot to determine who the potter was, they did gather some interesting data on the potters of Bé. At the time of their study in 1969–1970, there were ten potters in the village, all of whom were women who made their pots by molding and coiling and firing them in an open fire. Pottery making is a part-time activity carried out unwillingly by the relatively poor in order to earn enough to buy a few minor luxuries. Of the ten potters, seven were Fulani, two were Gisiga from 110 km away, and one was a Lame who immigrated from a chiefdom c. 100 km from Bé. Between the three

---

1. Several factors may contribute to the low percentage of Bé-produced ware in the sample. Because of the mobility of the potters, the number of potters in any one village is liable to vary irregularly. Villages will at some times be net exporters of ceramics and at other times they will be net importers. At the time of the survey, David and Hennig noted that Bé was 'almost self-sufficient' in pottery production, 'after a generation as a net importer' (1972:21, 22). Another consideration is the low quality of Bé-produced ware. Fulani women do not produce pottery until middle age when they are 'driven to the trade'; they work only occasionally, and they are 'satisfied by a narrow range of technically inferior and carelessly decorated wares'. Better-quality pottery is made by the Fali tribe and is available at a market only 22 km away (1972: 25-26).

groups of potters (Fulani, Gisiga and Lame), there is a considerable difference in technique and decorative motifs.

On one occasion during the study, the daughter of a Fulani villager made pottery while visiting her father (1972:4, 6). David and Hennig learned that no less than one-third of the pots made at Bé over the last 20 years were made by visitors to the village. In the dry season there are few essential tasks to be done so this is the ideal time for visits to relatives. It is also the best time for making pottery, so some of the visitors turn their leisure time to advantage and earn enough to buy presents for their hosts and families (1972:22).

Of the seven Fulani potters, two were trained at Bé, left, and subsequently returned, two were trained at a village 10 km away, one came from a village 30 km away, and two moved to Bé from 40 km distant. Of the ten potters active at Bé in 1969–1970, only three were resident there in 1966, and three had already left by November 1971 (1972:5, 21). Presumably, a similar pattern obtained in other pottery-producing villages in the region.[1]

I are not suggesting that the potters of ancient Palestine were as mobile as those of Bé, but the Bé example illustrates the diverse cultural and regional influences that can be present in the ceramic population of a small peasant village (cf. Kramer 1985:83) and also how these influences will tend to amalgamate and form a homogeneous style over a large region. One can also see the futility of any attempt to treat mathematically the diffusion of ceramic styles in North Cameroon on the basis of the archaeological record alone (p. 54 n. 2 above).

---

1. A contributing factor to the continual movement of the potters is the instability of the Fulani household. Fulani women go to live with their husbands in the same or in another, perhaps distant, village. A woman may migrate with her husband from place to place and may divorce and remarry several times. Twenty percent of Fulani women are divorced and remarried within two years of their first marriage and the average Fulani housewife is living with her third husband (1972:5, 23, 24).

Trends toward Standardization

The shape of a pottery vessel is related to its function, as opposed to decoration which is related to the aesthetic sensibilities of the culture (Rice 1987:207-42). As a result, vessel shapes are limited to those that meet a particular functional need (Kelso and Thorley 1943:98; Reina and Hill 1978:24-25; M. Smith 1985). Functional requirements therefore, plus cultural conformity (see below), tend to standardize ceramic shapes.

In addition, mass-production tends to promote standardization, as pointed out by Rathje (1975:430; cf. Kelso and Thorly 1943:98, 120; van der Leeuw 1981:375; Rice 1984:47-48; Longacre, Knamme and Kobayashi 1988). The fact that there were many production centers located close together in ancient Palestine tended to make this standardization uniform across the country (van der Leeuw 1981:375). Similarly, Ehrich observes that the use of the potter's wheel leads to a uniformity of style (1965:9). This standardization results in the formation of a 'mental template', i.e. a single dominant conception upon which all of the vessels within a class are patterned (Deetz 1967:45-49 *et passim*).

Potters learn pottery styles by observing other potters at work and also by observing the finished products of other potters. Stanislawski and Stanislawski observed how Hopi Indian potters learned ceramic style. They discovered that learning was a matter of imitation rather than the result of direct teaching. There were no 'trade secrets' and anyone was free to learn the craft (1978:75). Bunzel also studied the Hopi potters and found that if a new style became a commercial success, it was quickly adopted by other potters (1929:83).

The standardization and uniformity of ceramic style throughout Palestine obviously resulted from an intense interaction between potters, pottery and the buying community in a particular geo-political/ethnic region. Such interaction is the consequence of diffusion, which is of two types: expansion diffusion and relocation diffusion. In expansion diffusion, information or culture traits spread through a region while still remaining in their area of origin, while relocation diffusion is the spread of information or culture traits by carriers who move through new areas (Clarke 1978:426). We now turn to the question of the relative roles of each of these two types of diffusion as they affect the pottery repertoire of ancient Palestine.

Expansion Diffusion of Ceramic Style

Pottery brought into an area by merchants or by relocating consumers exposes the potter to the work of potters from areas far removed from his own. This tends to bring styles of different areas into conformity (Hodder 1978:260). Reina and Hill noted that, in Guatemala, potters are interested in the work of other potters, even their ancient counterparts (1978:21).

As a result of his work on Iroquois ceramic assemblages, Engelbrecht concludes that trade contacts and ceramic uniformity go hand-in-hand (1974:61). Rands notes that in the case of Palenque, stylistic patterns spread even beyond the area of trade contact (1967:150).

Thus, as ceramic vessels are diffused from the various places of manufacture, styles tend to harmonize. That ceramic vessels were widely dispersed in ancient Palestine is graphically illustrated by imported ware. Studies of the distribution of Mycenaean and Cypriote pottery in Palestine in the Late Bronze Age (Stubbings 1951; Hankey 1967; Leonard 1976; 1987; Gittlen 1975, 1977, 1981) demonstrate that a mechanism existed for distributing ceramic wares throughout the country.[1] These wares, or their contents (Gittlen 1981:55; Leonard 1981), were highly prized, as is indicated by their frequent occurrence in cultic and funerary contexts (Gittlen 1981:52; Hankey 1981). Emerging archaeological data indicate that locally-produced wares, even though they lacked a corresponding intrinsic value, were likewise dispersed widely throughout the country.

Ethnographic studies of preindustrial pottery-using cultures are unanimous in demonstrating that the primary means by which ordinary household pottery is diffused is by direct commercial sale by itinerant merchants. A secondary means is by relocating consumers. Additional modes of diffu-

---

1. This mechanism and how it functioned, however, has not been studied (Gittlen 1981:56; Nicolaou 1982:122).

sion for vessels containing goods, at least in antiquity (documented ethnographic examples are lacking), were by commercial trading and state provisioning.

Commercial Sale of Ceramic Wares. Investigators have given
little consideration to the fact that common pottery is transported over considerable distances in peasant societies through
trade (Nicklin 1971:14, 47). A visible example of such trade in
ancient Palestine is that of Philistine ware in the Iron I period
(12th–11th centuries BCE). Early in the 12th century BCE a
foreign group known as the Philistines settled on the southwest coastal region of Palestine. The settlers soon began fabricating a distinctive painted pottery which has affinities mainly
with Mycenaean ware, but also with Cypriote and Egyptian
ware (T. Dothan 1982:94-218). This pottery has been found at
numerous sites in Palestine, many of which are far removed
from Philistine territory (see fig. 17).

Petrographic analysis of Philistine pottery from Tell 'Aitun
and Beth-Shemesh shows that it was fabricated in the coastal
region (Edelstein and Glass 1973). Edelstein and Glass conclude that 'the Philistine pottery found at the excavations in
the Judean hills was brought there by traders' (1973:xvi).
Concerning the diffusion of Philistine pottery, T. Dothan
believes that its appearance outside the area of Philistine settlement is due to political or commercial activity (1982:217; cf.
Brug 1985:106).

In this case, we have pottery made by a foreign group, who
were, according to biblical traditions, on less than friendly
terms with the indigenous populace, being dispersed as far
north as Tel Dan, some 165 km from Philistine territory, and
as far east as Deir 'Allā, c. 85 km from Philistine territory.
Conversely, neutron activation analysis of a large sample (223
pieces) of Iron I pottery from Ashdod, one of the major Philistine centers, indicates that all of the pottery was locally made,
including Myc. IIIC:1 ware, Philistine ware, and indigenous
'Canaanite' ware (Asaro, Perlman and Dothan 1971; Perlman and Asaro 1982).[1]

1. These results indicate that Philistine ware was exported, but
Canaanite ware was not imported. This may be considered to be an

Ethnographic studies of pottery production in pre-industrial peasant societies where potters produce primarily for commercial sale have yielded much valuable information on the diffusion of common domestic wares.[1] These wares are widely dispersed (Arnold 1985:110; Okpoko 1987:454).[2] On the basis of his studies of the marketing of traditional pottery in Spain and Morocco, Vossen has determined that the distance pottery is traded from its production center is dependent upon eight factors (1984:362, 364):

1. The means of transportation
2. The geography of the region
3. The price of the pottery
4. The quality of the pottery
5. The traditional preferences of the customers
6. The amount of competition
7. Politically determined trade advantages or barriers
8. Social relations

anomaly which would be atypical for other periods, since the Philistines were a recently arrived foreign group with an apparent hostile proclivity toward the indigenous population (Judg. 13–16; 1 Sam. *passim*).

1. Ceramic distribution systems, however, have rarely been the subject of systematic ethnographic research (Kramer 1985:82, 96). For a discussion of the various mechanisms involved, see Rice 1987:191-200.

2. Specialized wares travel even further. Attic ware, for example, was distributed throughout the Mediterranean basin by traders in the Classical Period (Boardman 1979). Another example is the glazed pottery produced by the Tonque Pueblo in New Mexico in the 15th and 16th centuries CE. Here, in an area poorly suited to agriculture, a large ceramic industry and trading center thrived for nearly 200 years because its skilled potters had access to a high quality clay deposit and other essential mineral resources. Trading of this pottery dominated the economy of the Middle Rio Grande pueblos in an area c. 50 × 80 km. It has been found 130 km to the south, 240 km to the west and was also traded to the Plains Indians to the east in Texas, Kansas and Oklahoma (Warren 1969). Another example is Mexican Bruñida ware (1650–1810) which has been found 490 airline km from where it was produced (Charlton and Katz 1979:53). Elaborate wares being sold in the markets in Teotihucán Valley, Mexico, come from as far away as 320 km (Charlton 1976:145).

The existence of markets is the major driving force for the diffusion of ceramic wares in peasant societies. As Foster has observed:

> Given a market, animals or boats, and reasonably peaceful conditions, pottery of recognized quality can easily be traded up to 150 miles by the makers or original sellers before lesser distribution may carry it to more remote places (1965:56).[1]

The gap in our knowledge of village markets in the Middle East has been partially filled by Larson's excellent study of contemporary markets in Egypt (1982; cf. Herr 1988, based on ethnographic analogies from Asia and Africa). Village markets in Egypt are located along the streets of a village or held on the outskirts of a village or town on a plot of land officially set aside for the market. There is a tendency for sellers of the same goods to cluster together in one area of the market. Occasionally there are stalls of mud brick for the vendors, but usually they spread their goods on the ground together with other sellers of the same kind of goods. As a result, the market is divided into separate zones of activity. By noon most of the goods have been sold. The consumers return to their daily tasks while the vendors replenish their stocks in preparation for the next day's market in a nearby town (Larson 1982:131-32). Such activity would leave little evidence for the archaeologist to utilize in identifying a given area as a market.

Larson found that village markets are usually held only one day a week, with markets in neighboring villages being held on different days of the week. Not every village has a market, but markets are plentiful enough so that there is always one within easy reach. The number of weekly markets relative to population size is about one for every 36,000 people in northern Egypt and about one for every 30,000 people in southern Egypt. The distance between local markets is not more than 5 km in northern Egypt and c. 8 km in the south. At least 10 km separates the villages having markets on the same day in the

---

1. Note that the distance from Dan to Beersheba is 153 airline miles (245 km), so that in a small geographical region such as Palestine it would not be difficult for pottery from any one production center to be traded almost anywhere in the country.

south, while in the north markets meeting on the same day
may be as close as 4–5 km (1982:132-33).

In Palestine a number of weekly markets can still be
observed today. On Thursdays, for example, one can shop at
the camel market in Beersheba, although one is hard pressed
to find a camel for sale these days! A sheep market is held in
Jerusalem every Friday, outside the northeast corner of the
Old City wall.

Larson observed that pottery is one of the common craft
items for sale in rural Egyptian markets (1982: Table 1). In
Morocco, pottery is sold through a well-organized market
system that is centuries old (Vossen 1984:367-69). The products of village potters in Cyprus are sold through markets as
well (Taylor and Tufnell 1930:122; cf. Johnston 1974b:133).
The women potters of Darfur, Sudan, carry their products to
market on their backs (Haaland 1978:55). In the pottery-
making community of Tzintzuntzan, Mexico, the wares are
sold in a local market 16 km away. In 1945, men and women
drove pack mules and burros laden with pots, although it was
beginning to be realized that trucks and buses offered cheaper
transportation. At the market, the potters of Tzintzuntzan
complete with 200–300 other potters, some from as far away
as 220 km (Foster 1965:45).

The most thorough study of the marketing of ceramics is
that done by Reina and Hill for Guatemala. Between 1973 and
1975 they documented the distribution of pottery over the
entire country. The topography of Guatemala is similar to that
of Palestine. It consists of three major regions: the lowlands,
including the Pacific coast, 30–65 km wide; the Pacific piedmont, c. 30 km wide, and the highlands. The Pacific coast area
is c. 240 km long and 24 km wide with a sparse population.
The Pacific piedmont is a transitional zone between the coastal
lowlands and the highlands. It is from 200 to 900 m in elevation and is heavily eroded by rivers cutting across it. The
highlands, divided into the western, central, eastern and
northern highlands, are from 900 to 1800 m in elevation.[1] The
central highlands, a mountainous land with deep valleys and a

1. This compares with 450–900 m for the central hill country of Palestine.

semi-tropical climate, is the most densely populated area of the country (Reina and Hill 1978:4-7). Roads and trails link towns and villages in the central highlands, but the people live in relative cultural isolation following the dictates of their various community cultures. The marketplace, however, serves to bring the people together for economic transactions, including the buying and selling of pottery (1978:29).

Pottery production is carried out in the highland zone by small rural population units ('production centers') which are politically and economically dependent on much larger towns. There is a hierarchy of pottery distribution in Guatemala composed of two interrelated networks: the pottery district and the pottery region. A pottery district is a network formed by a regional market and the nearby production centers that supply it in areas where transportation systems are poorly developed. A pottery region, on the other hand, is a network composed of a production center or group of centers supplying a regional market or group of regional markets in areas of well-developed transportation systems. Pottery distribution networks cut across most environmental and cultural boundaries, including political and ethnic boundaries (1978:216).

There are three levels of markets for pottery distribution: local, regional and interregional; similarly, there are three types of sellers: vendors, middlemen and merchants. The vendors are people who sell their own pottery or the pottery made by a member of their immediate family; they are most active in local markets. The middlemen provide the link between the vendor and the merchant and work in both the local and regional market.[1] The merchants purchase bulk quantities of pottery directly from the vendors or, more often, from middlemen, and sell the wares in markets along a specific route (1978:207).

Local markets in pottery-producing areas supply pottery for local needs as well as supplying pottery to merchants for export. In either case, it is sold by the vendor. The local market is usually held once or twice a week. On a typical day, the San Cristóbal Totonicapán local market had 11 vendors, each with

---

1. Middlemen have also been noted in Africa (Nicklin 1971:13; Okpoko 1987: 454).

an inventory of over 20 vessels; one had an inventory of 75 vessels. All of them, nine women and two men, had come to the market on foot to sell their own products. The price of the pots was from five to 50 cents in 1974, depending on size. Merchants in San Cristóbal Totonicapán buy their pottery through a middleman, who has a contractual arrangement with local producers. In local markets outside the pottery-producing areas, where there are no vendors, pottery is imported by merchants. These merchants limit their stock to an inventory acceptable to their clientele (1978:209, 211, 212, 215).

The regional market takes in wares from a number of production centers and sets the pattern for distribution on a national scale because of its role as intermediary between the production centers and the country as a whole. In regional markets middlemen and merchants are the strongest economic group as opposed to the vendors at the local market. The distribution of pottery by merchants in regional markets is carefully related to custom. Boundaries for given types of vessels are clear and the forms are, by cultural definition, stable (1978:215-16, 238, 242).

There are a few regional markets that supply two or three regions. Guatemala City is the only national inter-regional market for the transshipment of products to all regions of the country. Hundreds of producers from nearby production centers come weekly to sell their vessels. The Mercado La Terminal in Guatemala City serves as a warehouse for pottery. From there, pottery is transshipped throughout the country through a complex network of middlemen. Using modern transportation, these middlemen serve a complicated and socially heterogeneous population with pottery to suit each segment of the nation (1978:219, 225). The pottery from one production center, Chinautla, for example, is distributed throughout the western part of the country, to the western border 180 km away (1978: map 9).

The production cycle of pottery workshops in Morocco is determined by the weekly market (figs. 19, 21).

At sundown the evening before market day, the kilns are fired. The entire process, including loading, cooling time, etc., takes only a few hours. Early in the morning the newly-fired vessels are loaded onto pack animals. Between 7 and 9 a.m. the potters arrive at the market and set out their wares in the section reserved for potters, next to the pottery dealers and often in the neighborhood of the charcoal makers or dealers. Depending upon the size of the market and the season, there may be as many as 25 pottery vendors at a typical Moroccan market. Vessels which the vendors are unable to sell directly to consumers are sold to pottery dealers at a wholesale price (Vossen 1984:369-70).

The potters also use the visit to the market as an opportunity to do family shopping, visit the barber, exchange news in the tea-house and stock up on supplies. There is usually no work done in the workshop on market day. The next day, clay and fuel supplies are replenished and clay is prepared. On the second day, production begins for the next market day (1984:370).

Conditioned by the rhythm of the market cycle, the output of a small family shop in Morocco is not large. Depending upon the type and size of vessel being produced, and the manufacturing process, between 30 and 200 pots are turned out per week, or between 1500 and 10,000 per year. This cycle may be interrupted by unfavorable weather, illness in the family, or holidays. There also may be times when it is more profitable to fire a larger number of vessels every two or three weeks and visit a more distant market where prices are higher or where the potential for sales is greater (1984).

Potters themselves are responsible for some of the movement of pottery as they carry their wares from the production site to market. Likewise, consumers move the pottery further afield when they take their vessels, newly acquired at the market, to their homes. Generally, however, this only accounts for the diffusion of ceramics in a localized region around the production center. It is the itinerant merchant who is the prime mover of products in a peasant society and who is responsible for the diffusion of merchandise over wide areas. These merchants transport goods, including pottery, great distances, hawking their wares from market to market and village to village as they move along their route.

The role of the itinerant pottery merchant is best documented for Guatemala. There, they move in specific routes and tie together different areas of the country in a distribution system. Vessels are loaded into a special back frame and carried on foot by means of a tumpline.

The amount traded is determined by what an individual can carry. Motorized transport, however, is now replacing the backpack system (1984:207).[1]

R.H. Thompson describes the construction of a back frame used in the Yucatan Peninsula, Mexico (1958:101-5). An average frame holds six to twelve large pots and many more smaller ones.[2] Merchants carry the frames by means of a tumpline and sell the wares throughout the Yucatan Peninsula.

In Egypt, pottery from Qena is brought 70 km on donkeyback and sold in the Luxor region, while pottery made in Luxor is taken by boat as far south as Aswan, a trip of over 200 km (Brissaud 1982:184, 185). The Ballas jar made in Deir el-Gharbi, Upper Egypt, is distributed by middlemen throughout Egypt, from Cairo to Aswan (Nicholson and Patterson 1985:233). Villagers of Aliabad, in the Zagros mountains of Iran, obtain their pottery from itinerant merchants who transport their wares on donkey-back. The pottery probably originates in a small industrial village c. 20 km away (Kramer 1982:42, 113).

Annis and Geertman (1987) describe the distribution of wares produced in Pabillonis, southwest Sardinia, for the period 1930–1950. This specialized production center produced a cooking pot and a casserole that were used throughout the island. Three modes of distribution were operative. In the immediate vicinity of Pabillonis, women, usually working in pairs, distributed the pots on foot. They purchased wholesale lots and stored them in their homes, selling on alternate days throughout most of the year. A normal day's load consisted of eight pots, carried in head baskets. The women hawked their wares door-to-door, up to a maximum range of 20 km (1987:165-67).

1. In some areas, mules are used rather than the backpack. For documented examples of the travels of itinerant merchants in Guatemala, see Reina and Hill 1978:41, 64, 69, 86-87, 92, 103, 117-18, 127, 130, 141, 152, 154, 171, 176, 181, 185.
2. Cf. Whitaker and Whitaker 1978: fig. 52. Wissler (1946:330) shows a back frame loaded with scores of pots.

The second category of middleman was the full-time itinerant merchant. He would first deliver consignments of pots by horse-drawn cart to strategic points along a specified route. These redistribution centers were in the homes of acquaintances, where the merchant would also spend the night. The cart was returned to Pabillonis and the actual selling done on foot. The merchant was away from home several weeks at a time, often more than a month, selling a total of 400–480 pots. The entire island was serviced in this manner, up to 135 km from the production center (1987:167-70). A few wholesalers were involved in the distribution of Pabillonis cooking ware. They placed large quantities of pots in depots in the central and northern parts of the island, and from there they redistributed the ware to other middlemen (1987:170).

In Spain, pottery is sold by merchants from burro-back over great distances. Some 100 families in Salvatierra de los Barros make their living as itinerant pottery merchants. In the 1930s and 1940s these merchants were organized into groups of four to five men each. The groups travelled with 15–20 mules loaded with pottery throughout Spain and into France and Germany. Today, they use trucks to transport their wares to centralized depots. From there, they sell to the surrounding countryside using donkeys. The pottery is marketed in this fashion up to 400 km from Salvatierra de los Barros (Vossen 1984:343-45).

Before the turn of the century, pottery manufactured in Agost, Spain, was traded against its content in grain, flour, eggs, almonds or oil in surrounding provinces. Such exchanges were governed by certain proportions depending upon the value of the commodity (1984:354-55). Between 1920 and 1936, 14–20 middlemen sold pottery using carts. Each cart, which could hold seven to ten times the load of a single donkey, was drawn by three to four donkeys harnessed in single file. One typical merchant travelled to markets as far away as 175 km, averaging 40–50 km per day with his donkey cart (1984:358).

Women retailers specializing in the pottery trade in Ghana disseminate pottery a considerable distance by foot. They travel from neighboring villages to production centers where they buy a consignment of pots. The wares are head-loaded in sacks containing six to twelve pots and transported along numerous footpaths radiating from the production centers. Foot transport is preferred since poor roads result in a high breakage rate when motorized transport is used. The estimated range of these enterprising merchants is c. 50 km east and 60 km south (Crossland and Posnausky 1978:87). Pottery made in Simbila, Peru, is sold as far as the Ecuadorian border, some 200 km distant as the crow flies (Bankes 1985:275).

Full-time muleteers in Tzintzuntzan, Mexico, carry pottery and other merchandise to distant points. Some of the potters engage in muleteering, as do others who split this occupation with other forms of work. At the time of his observations in 1945, Foster determined that there was one muleteer for every five pottery-making families in Tzintzuntzan. Most muleteers made trips of not more than a week on regular schedules, usually to market towns where either clays are not good for pottery or where people prefer to work at other things. The longest trips were to the Pacific coast, c. 240 km distant, requiring about a month for the round trip. On these journeys, muleteers worked more or less like tramp steamers, picking up and selling local cargo as they worked along their trade route (Foster 1965:45).

Arnold lists the advantages of dealing with a merchant to the potters of Quinua, Peru: (1) the potters do not have to transport their pottery beyond the village, (2) they can sell all of it at the same time and eliminate separate trips to one or more markets, and (3) they are frequently paid in advance on consignment (1972:871).

In a sophisticated economy, the relationship between the itinerant merchant and the potter can become extremely complex. Van der Leeuw cites an example from Temascalcingo, Mexico, where the potters are totally controlled by pottery traders (1977:73). The traders determine not only the price to be paid for the pottery, but also the price the potter has to pay for his necessities (which have to be bought at the trader's store) and his firewood (which is brought from afar on the trader's trucks). Since the price paid for the pottery is extremely low, the potter's life depends upon his ability to produce large numbers of vessels, which in turn leads to narrow specialization.

Among island and coastal cultures, pottery is carried great distances by boat. In the LB I period, pottery from mainland Greece was distributed in the Cyclades, apparently by merchants (Cherry and Davis 1982). Mallowan (1939) cites a contemporary example of trading amphorae by ship along the Mediterranean coast. Jars made in Sidon were transported to el Bôss in Syria, some 240 km north, and traded for dung. Large ships would carry 1000–1500 jars, while a smaller ship would carry 200–400. The exchange rate was two amphorae for one donkey load (one sack) of dung. The dung, in turn, was sold in various port towns, particularly Tripoli, where it was in great demand as fertilizer. Domestic wares are distributed throughout the Aegean by small boats today as they were in antiquity (Casson 1938:466; 1951:190; Matson 1972:213).

Large oil jars made on the island of Djerba in southern Tunisia are exported hundreds of kilometers to Libya, up the Tunisian coast and into Algeria (Peacock 1981:191; Balfet 1981:264). Similarly, the pottery of Nabeul, Tunisia, is distributed throughout these same regions by pottery dealers (Lisse and Louis 1956:221). The Motu on the south coast of New Guinea export thousands of pots each year by canoe and foot along the shores of the Papuan Gulf and in the immediate hinterland. Annually, the Motu make voyages of c. 240 km across the Papuan Gulf to sell pottery. Between 1954 and 1958 Groves observed a number of these expeditions preparing to embark; thousands of vessels were taken each time, with one expedition taking c. 10,000 pots for trade (1960:8-10). Nicklin cites similar examples from various regions, the most noteworthy being in Africa where pots are transported 320 km up the Benue River in Nigeria and 500 km along the east African coast (1971:15).

A Proposed Model for the Commercial Sale of Ceramic Wares in Ancient Palestine. Since the commercial sale of ceramic wares was the major way in which household pottery was diffused in ancient Palestine, we wish to explore this subject in greater depth and propose a model by which this type of diffusion took place. Ethnographic data is of paramount importance in developing such a model (Hodder 1978:199).

The hypothesis which we propose is that ceramic styles diffused primarily as a result of the distribution of ceramic wares through a marketing system as has been observed in various primitive economies (above). The hypothesis consists of three major postulates:

Postulate 1 Pottery was produced in urban centers as an urban craft specialization.

Postulate 2 Markets existed in each urban center and its satellite villages, and the pottery was marketed in these outlets by the producers themselves and also by merchants, thus diffusing wares within the orbit of the urban center.

Postulate 3 Itinerant merchants diffused the wares even further by transporting them to adjacent urban center markets and beyond.

The archaeological data thus far support the validity of Postulate 1. There has been little work done on village sites, however, so that at this point we cannot rely on archaeological evidence alone.[1] The basis of Postulate 1 is largely the socio-economic system of Palestine in the Bronze and Iron Ages. During much of that period the primary socio-economic system was that of a city-state, that is, a major urban center surrounded by satellite villages. Since an urban center is an administrative and cultic center, pottery production associated with these levels of the social structure would be carried out here. The best potters were no doubt employed by the cultic

---

1. Several village sites have recently been excavated: Tell Qiri and Tel Qashish in the Jezreel Valley (Ben-Tor and Portugali 1987; Ben-Tor, Portugali and Avissar 1981), Tel Yin'am in the southern Galilee (Liebowitz and Folk 1984; Liebowitz 1981) and Tell el-Hayyat in the Jordan Valley (Falconer, Metzer and and Magness-Gardiner 1984). Thus far, there has been no evidence for pottery manufacture at small villages during highly urbanized periods. Moreover, there is no difference in the type or quality of pottery at the village sites when compared with pottery from nearby urban centers (Ben-Tor and Portugali 1987:208-10, 224-35). Neutron-activation studies of pottery from the Jordan Valley in the Early Bronze–Middle Bronze transitional period, on the other hand, suggest that pottery manufacture during times of less intense urbanization was decentralized, with pottery being produced at both large and small villages (Falconer 1987).

72   *The Sociology of Pottery*

centers and royal administration. In addition to their own skills, presumably these potters would have access to the best available techniques through contacts with other urban centers and possibly even through foreign contacts,[1] so that the best pottery was produced by the cultic and royal potters.

The independent potters in the urban center would assimilate these skills and techniques through their close contact. The independent potters, in addition to producing a superior product, would have excellent marketing opportunities in the urban center itself and also in surrounding villages. This would not only ensure economic success, but would also result in a high-volume, low per-unit cost, operation. A village production center, on the other hand, would not have as wide a marketing base, and thus, unless it was specialized, would have difficulty maintaining an economically viable operation. Moreover, village centers probably would not be able to compete with their urban counterparts in terms of quality or unit price. Vossen postulates that a production center is required every 20 km in order to supply a population of 50–100 inhabitants per square km with utilitarian pottery (1984:371-73). This is approximately the distance between urban centers in ancient Palestine.

The sudden appearance of poorly-made pottery at village sites, such as in the Iron I period, would signal a fundamental change in the production–distribution system. It would no doubt reflect a breakdown of the social system, in which case the villages would be required to become independent and thus produce their own, poorer quality, ceramic wares. Brandfon (1981:107, 109) and Aharoni (1982:174) suggest that such a development may be the result of the arrival of new groups. Unless such groups were self-sufficient in pottery production, however, they would most likely purchase their ceramic wares at the local market, as did the indigenous population. A study of fabrication techniques in the Baq'ah valley in Transjordan indicates a continuous industrial tradition between the Late Bronze II period and the Iron I period (Glanzman and Fleming 1986: McGovern 1986).

1. This may be a moot point since techniques seem to remain relatively unchanged throughout the Bronze and Iron Ages.

The existence of markets, Postulate 2, hardly needs defense. Markets are a natural development in an agrarian society (Berry 1967:108; Hodder and Orton 1976:55, 76). On the basis of the universal observation that markets are a necessary part of a complex society, it is certain that a market system existed in ancient Palestine.[1] In the Galilee region, Meyers argues that the location of the city-states of the Late Bronze period indicates that they 'reflect an economic life in which a significant exchange of goods was a component', as opposed to the later Iron I sites which were self-sufficient (1983:52).

Dalton defines the economy of a political system with a centralized political authority, such as a city-state, as a 'primitive economy'. In addition to socio-economic transactions within the local community and between local communities, primitive economies have transactions between the political center and its satellite villages, and external trade transactions between the political centers and foreign centers (Dalton 1969:73).

The optimum distance between markets is c. 10 km, according to Hodder and Orton. Above this distance, the time and effort to get to market is too great, and below this distance, there is insufficient trade to sustain a market (Hodder and Orton 1976:57; cf. Larson's observations for rural Egypt, pp. 62-63 above).

Furthermore, some of these markets, such as those at coastal sites with good harbor facilities, may grow in importance to become regional or international trading centers (e.g. Joppa, Hopkins 1980:23-24). The impulse for such growth is of three kinds according to Hodder and Orton (1976:74, 76).

1. Long distance trade. Some markets may act as collecting points for the siphoning off of goods from internal networks and the articulation of these goods with external centers. They may also act as nodes for the redistribution of imports to surrounding areas.
2. Regional interface. Markets located on boundaries between ecological zones may become involved with the exchange of differing products of adjacent areas.

1. For evidence for the existence of markets in the ancient Near East, see Silver 1985:118-21.

3. Political or tribal interface. Markets located on political or tribal boundaries may participate in external exchange, particularly when there is some cultural or ecological variety between the groups.

The situation in Guatemala is much like one would expect to find in ancient Palestine. Geographical variation has created many small ecological zones suitable for particular agricultural or commercial specialization. Although communities may have distinctive cultural variations, and may be socially closed entities, members meet in a socially unbounded atmosphere in the market. Markets in Guatemala are located in socially neutral areas, usually in the center of a town, near the church and main plaza, where people with products meet in an organized fashion. The market organizes time, furnishes a livelihood for many thousands of people and provides an interlude in an otherwise wearisome routine (Reina and Hill 1978:207).

The network of markets in ancient Palestine, therefore, provided an outlet for the distribution of ceramic wares over a considerable distance. The importance of the connection between markets and ceramic diffusion has been emphasized by Foster:

> Markets explain the diffusion of the same pottery over wide areas; and a range of at least 150 miles from the source, carried by the producer or original middleman, is recorded in widely separated parts of the world (1965:59).

Although markets provide the outlets for the sale of pottery, it is the itinerant merchant, Postulate 3, who accounts for the diffusion of ceramic wares over large distances (Renfrew 1975:43). The itinerant merchant is an important part of a primitive economy, as we have seen from the ethnographic examples above, and certainly he was operative in ancient Palestine. He is attracted by a situation in which there are many potteries in a given area, as was the case in ancient Palestine (Part I above), because he can deal with large numbers of vessels and thereby make a sufficient profit (Peacock 1982:9; cf. 1981:190).

In ancient Palestine, the pottery salesman was the middleman between the producer and the consumer. He bought pots in quantity and sold them wherever he could, transporting his merchandise by foot or donkey (Dorsey 1988:894-95)[1] along the roads that connected the urban centers and their satellite villages,[2] or by boat along the coast. Knowing where the markets are, and which days they are open, allows the itinerant merchant to establish a profitable itinerary (Hodder and Orton 1976:61).[3]

Curtis (1962:500) reports on a chance encounter with an itinerant pottery merchant on the road to Segovia, Spain, a town 105 km northwest of Madrid. The merchant was walking slowly along the road beside his packed burro which was loaded down with bowls of various sizes, water jars and a few flower pots. They were lashed together inside a twig, wire and string sling tied together with rope, protected here and there from contact with each other by loose straw. He stopped at a farmhouse where, after intense bargaining, he sold the farmer's wife a set of four bowls.

Upon inquiry, Curtis learned that the merchant was from Bailén where the wares were made, some 400 km to the south. He arranged to have wares sent by truck as he needed them to various focal points from which he covered the provinces. At the time of the encounter he made his headquarters in Segovia. From there he and two assistants, each with a burro, covered the immediate area, returning to Segovia to replenish their stock. After covering an area, he would return to Bailén, visit with his family, and arrange for a new shipment to some

---

1. Overland trade at Ugarit was by means of donkeys (Cornelius 1981:22).

2. On roads in ancient Palestine, see Aharoni 1979:43-63; Har-El 1981; Dorsey forthcoming.

3. On the role of the merchant in a peasant society, see Halligan 1983:18. The words used most often in the Old Testament for the activity of a merchant, *sāḥar* (15 times), *rākal* (15 times) and *tûr* (twice), mean 'to travel about'. 'Canaanite' is used five times in the sense of merchant. The texts from Ugarit speak a great deal about the merchant who was in service to the king (see the useful summary of Cornelius, 1981:15-19, and references there). The royal merchant was involved in international commerce, so these texts are of little help in illuminating the role of the pottery merchant who was involved in local and regional trade. On merchants in general, see Polyani 1975.

other large city where he would start afresh. He stated that he spent many months on each trip and was seldom home.

To test our proposed model for the commercial sale of ceramic wares, large-scale provenience studies are required. It would be necessary to subject a large sample of local Palestinian wares from an urban center to neutron-activation analysis, along with a large sample from a contemporary stratum of a satellite village.[1] The urban production center/itinerant merchant diffusion model would then predict the following results:

a. The largest percentage of urban center pottery would be locally made.

b. A significant percentage of the urban center pottery would originate in areas beyond the urban center, with the percentage varying inversely with the travel-time from the center.

c. The largest percentage of the village sample would have a trace-element profile similar to that of the locally-made urban center wares.

d. A significant percentage of the village sample would originate from areas outside the urban center, with the percentage varying inversely with the travel-time from the village.

Although such a large-scale neutron-activation analysis study has not been carried out for the Bronze and Iron Ages, Brooks *et al.* conducted a similar study on Tell el-Hesi samples from the Persian period (6th–4th centuries BCE) and Gezer samples from various (unspecified) periods (1974). The results tend to support the model outlined above. The largest percentage of the pottery at these two urban sites was locally made, while a significant percentage originated in areas beyond the urban center (table 1; cf. Yellin and Gunneweg 1985; Gunneweg *et al.* 1986; Sharon, Yellin and Perlman 1987: 232-33; Falconer 1987).

1. Such provenience studies have been conducted for Palenque, Mexico (Rands 1967); Tonque Pueblo, New Mexico (Warren 1969); Tikal, Guatemala (Fry and Cox 1974; Fry 1979, 1980) and the southeast Maya region (Beaudry 1984).

With regard to satellite villages, samples from sites neighboring Hesi, for the most part, matched the local field clay and/or mud brick and 'the materials and clays from the different sites could not be significantly differentiated through composition' (*ibid.* 57, 62). This observation supports the contention that the majority of the pottery of satellite villages was produced at the urban center. The pottery excavated at the village sites of Qiri Qashish and Yin'am appears in all respects to be identical to the pottery from nearby urban centers (p. 71 n. 1 above).

Bullard conducted petrographic analyses of pottery from Gezer and concluded that at least eight clay sources are represented (1970:107-108):

Type I	immediate area around Gezer
Type II	lowlands immediately north and east of Gezer
Type III	Shephelah to the north and the Judean mountains to the east
Type IV	basalt areas such as Galilee
Type V	Aijalon Valley, Yarkon River valley and the Sorek Valley
Type VI	coastal plain
Type VII	an area with volcanic material, possibly the Golan
Type VIII	unknown clay sources

Bullard's work was not comprehensive enough to provide percentages of the various types, but it again demonstrates the diverse origins of the ceramic population at a typical Palestinian urban center.

Secondary Agencies for the Expansion Diffusion of Ceramic Wares. Secondary means of dispersing ceramic wares throughout the area were by commercial container traffic, state container traffic and the movement of consumers.

Commercial container traffic would of course involve only closed vessels which were used to transport such consumables as beverages (wine, beer), oils, aromatics, unguents, etc. The Mycenaean ware which reached the eastern shores of the Mediterranean in the LB II period was probably used for this type of trade (Leonard 1981). Such goods would have been sold through markets by itinerant merchants in much the same way as household pottery discussed above. Three Iron II store jars with identical potter's marks found at Beersheba, Tell esh-Shari'a and Lachish (Yadin 1974:34; 1976:6) may attest to commercial container traffic. If these distinctive marks (two horizontal triangles joined at the apex) were made by the same potter, then it is likely that all three jars were fabricated at a common location. In that case they would have been shipped to the other sites, c. 40–50 km distant.[1]

Neutron-activation analysis has shown that of 22 Iron I store jars excavated at Tel Dan, six (27%) were locally made, while the remaining 16 were imported from seven different (unidentified) geographical regions (Yellin and Gunneweg 1989). Hole-mouth pithoi fabricated in the Jerusalem area were transported to Beersheba (81 km), Arad (100 km) and Kuntillet 'Ajrud (c. 225 airline km) in the Iron II period (Gunneweg, Perlman and Meshel 1985: Table 1). A similar pithos fabricated from Ashdod clay was found in Arad, some 150 km distant (*ibid.*). In addition, the study determined that a number of store jars found in an early eighth-century BCE context at Kuntillet 'Ajrud came from the southern coastal region, c. 210 airline km away (1985). The work of Hennessy and Millett (1963), Amiran and Glass (1979), Åström and Jones (1982), and Gunneweg, Perlman and Asaro (1987; Mazar 1988) demonstrate that locally produced containers traveled far beyond the borders of Palestine as part of international commerce.

Sites in southern Palestine have yielded a large number of jar handles from Iron II contexts which bear a unique stamp. It is composed of three elements: (1) the inscription *lmlk*, meaning 'to the king', (2) one of four place names—Hebron, Ziph, Socoh, or *mmšt*,[2] and (3) an insignia of either a four-

---

1. An alternative explanation is that the potter who fabricated the jars traveled from site to site making the jars on the spot. This, however, seems unlikely since each of these urban sites would have had its own ceramic industry. I am indebted to John S. Holladay, Jr, for bringing this example to my attention.

2. Ziph is located at Tel Zif (Rainey 1982:59) and Socoh at Shuweika (Amiran [Kallner] and Vroman 1946; Rainey 1982:59; 1983:15) or Kh.

wing scarab or a two-wing sun disc. The handles come from large store jars[1] and are undoubtedly associated with a royal wine industry. Their presence at sites throughout the kingdom of Judah is possibly related to the provisioning of military forces and royal administrators (Na'aman 1986:12-13, 16-17). The inscription *lmlk* indicates royal property, the insignia probably represents a particular king and the place names indicate the winery from which the wine came (Cross 1969:20-22; Rainey 1982). The jars themselves, regardless of the place name on the stamp, were all fabricated at a single location somewhere in the Shephelah (Mommsen, Perlman and Yellin 1984).[2]

Distribution by the movement of consumers is an aspect of ceramic diffusion that is many times overlooked (Nicklin 1979:453-54). A polychrome ware identified as 'Midianite ware' found at a number of sites in Palestine appears to be an example of this type of diffusion (fig. 23).[3] It occurs in abundance in the south Arabah, particularly at Timna, where it can be dated to the 13th–12th centuries BCE on the basis of associated local ware and Egyptian scarabs (Rothenberg 1972:107-10; Rothenberg and Glass 1983:100-101). At other Palestinian sites it occurs only sporadically. Midianite ware was found to be the local and common pottery at Qurayyah in northwest Arabia c. 160 km southeast of Aqaba (Parr, Harding and Dayton 1970:240; Parr 1982:127-30) and subsequent petrographic analyses have verified this area as the source of the ceramic (Rothenberg 1972:163; Slatkine 1974:107-109; Kalsbeek and London 1978:49, 53; Rothenberg and Glass 1983:111-13). Here we have a striking illustration of how far pottery was transported in antiquity, with examples of this ware being

---

'Abbâd (Welten 1969: taf. III; Aharoni 1979:398; Na'aman 1986:12). *Mmšt* remains unidentified (Rainey 1982:59; Na'aman 1986:15).

1. A number of complete examples have been found at Lachish (Ussishkin 1976; 1977).

2. A similar example of inscribed jars associated with royal provisioning is Egyptian amphorae inscribed with hieratic labels known in the New Kingdom and Ramesside periods (Wood 1987).

3. For a technical description of the ware, see Dayton 1972:27 and Kalsbeek and London 1978.

found as far away as Amman, 600 km and a six-day camel march north of Qurayyah (Dayton 1972:29).

From the large sample at Timna, it appears that most of the Midianite pottery is kitchen and table ware of various types (Rothenberg and Glass 1983:115). It is speculated that the ware was brought from Arabia by workers skilled in metallurgy (Rothenberg and Glass 1981:81*; 1983:115).[1]

There are examples of similar movements of pottery in contemporary societies. In south Senegal, West Africa, for example, Linares de Sapir has noted a stylistic similarity in pottery north and south of the Casamace River, even though distinctive cultural groups, the Fogny and the Kasa, live in these regions. The similarity is largely due to the movement of people. The Fogny initially migrated north from the Kasa region. Then, in both areas standard forms and techniques were diffused, in one by the circulation of the women who made the pots and in the other by the circulation of the pots themselves (Linares de Sapir 1969:11).

Another example of this phenomenon is that of Bé cited above. Immigrants to this North Cameroon village carried household pottery a distance of 110 km. There can be little doubt that the people of antiquity were as mobile as their counterparts in contemporary peasant cultures, probably in response to economic conditions. The high mobility of the Fulani in North Cameroon (cf. David and Hennig) is because chiefs entice them into their chiefdoms by promising lower taxes and other benefits. A demographic sample of the Fulani revealed that 46 percent of the population no longer resided in the village in which they were born (David and Hennig 1972:3).

Binford favors the 'Big Man System' to explain the origin of complex society. In this system, chiefs offer economic security to their followers by means of alliances with other chiefs. When the support from these alliances is depleted, the people move on to other chiefdoms where there is a promise of greater security. The result of this type of system, notes Binford, is

---

1. For a bibliography on Midianite pottery see Brandl 1984.

an unending movement of population through the habitat in almost perfect adjustment to changing patterns of differential production (1983:219).

Binford's model applies particularly well to a city-state system, since each city-state was in effect controlled by a 'big man' (the king) who no doubt made alliances with other 'big men' in the region. During the Amarna period, peasants fled from cities where there was a food shortage to cities where there was grain (Halpern 1983:57-61, 88). As the populace moved through the habitat transferring allegiance from one 'big man' to another, their portable goods went with them.

Relocation Diffusion of Ceramic Style
The other major way in which ceramic style is diffused is by relocation diffusion, that is, the spread of style by potters who move into new areas. This can be the result of itinerant potting or a change of residence, either temporary or permanent.

Itinerant Potters. There is considerable evidence that itinerant potting is relatively common in peasant societies. Such a practice acts to diffuse ceramic styles since the itinerant potter himself provides a living demonstration of his techniques, and the vessels he leaves behind are enduring examples of those techniques. The itinerant potter, in turn, learns local styles as he travels from place to place. No doubt such activities were practiced in antiquity (Matson 1965:212), but we have no solid evidence to back this claim (Zaccagnini 1983:258).

Regarding pottery making in Cyprus, Casson notes that the potters follow ancient traditions, both in vessel shape and in methods of manufacture and distribution. Some of the potters are itinerant:

> They will set out with their donkey and with a load of pots for sale. They will also convey with them a consignment of wet clay. Arrived in a village they will sell pots ready made and also make pottery to commission. They will even mend damaged pots and partly remake others. They work on the spot and then move on (Casson 1938:467).

In Crete, Xanthoudides has documented the activities of a group of itinerant potters from Thrapsanos who tour the island for about three months in the summer (1927:118; cf. Voyatzoglou 1973, 1974). Johnston has observed this pattern in other areas of the Middle East (1974a:95) and Matson tells of wandering tribes in Ethiopia and Afghanistan who specialize in making pottery (1965:212).

There is also a group of itinerant potters in west Tibet who work from April to November, when the ground is soft enough for them to extract their clay. They go from village to village, where there is suitable clay, and make vessels to order. Payment is normally in kind (meals, flour, grain), or occasionally in money. They have formed a type of union in order to exclude others from engaging in the trade (Asboe 1946:10). In central Peru, travelling potters carry unfired clay with them and make pots to order along the way (Donnan 1971:464; cf. 1973:94-95).

Relocating Potters. As with itinerant potters, relocating potters take their knowledge and styles with them as they move into new areas. They are likewise influenced by any new techniques to which they are exposed (Vossen 1984:375). The free movement of potters will thus act to harmonize styles and technology over a large area.

In antiquity, craftsmen attached to city-states were extremely mobile. Royal potters may have been part of this movement. Based on textual evidence, Zaccagnini sees three main patterns of mobility among state craftsmen: redistributive, where artisans were moved about within the area controlled by the city state; reciprocative, where artisans were exchanged between different palace organizations (governed by the rules of gift exchange); and commercial, where artisans moved freely in the labor market (1983:247-64; cf. Gordon 1956:140). With the demise of Late Bronze Age culture and the breakdown of palace organization, Zaccagnini postulates that displaced craftsmen were reabsorbed into non-palace modes of production (1983:258). This would have resulted in additional movement of potters.

An excellent example of relocation diffusion from the archaeological record is that of Philistine potters. They were transplanted from their native country, probably somewhere in the Aegean (Dothan 1982:21-23), to the coast of Palestine early in the twelfth century BCE. They brought with them the technology they had practiced in their homeland. The first ware they produced in Palestine, Myc. IIIC:1 ware, is indistinguishable from Myc. IIIC:1 ware made in the Aegean.[1] Shortly thereafter, however, the Philistine potters introduced local elements, resulting in a hybrid pottery which soon supplanted the Myc. IIIC:1 ware (1982:96).

Philistine pottery is derived directly from the Myc. IIIC:1 style (Furumark 1972:118-22), but has additional Cypriote, Egyptian, and local Canaanite elements (Dothan 1982:94-218). It would appear that after the first generation of immigrant potters had passed away, their successors combined local traditions with what they had inherited from their forebears to produce what we call today 'Philistine' pottery.[2]

The relocation of contemporary village potters in the Levant is well attested (Johnston 1974a:95). Matson documents an example of a group of potters from the Aegean island of Siphnos who moved to Vounaria on the Greek mainland, stayed four or five years, and then left (1972:213).

Some of this movement is seasonal in nature. Matson notes that such movement 'can result in the wide distribution of ceramic styles, both in shape and decoration' (1974:345). Potters from Djerba, Tunisia, often migrate seasonally or permanently to other pottery centers in Tunisia (Lisse and Louis 1956:15; Combès and Louis 1967:25). In Afghanistan, Matson has observed the seasonal movement of potters from Julalabad to Kabul, 80 km distant, to spend the summer months each year. There, they make and sell large quantities of pottery. In the winter they return to Julalabad where they also make pottery (1974:345).

1. Neutron-activation analysis has demonstrated that the Myc. IIIC:1b ware found at Ashdod and Tel Miqne was locally produced (Asaro, Perlman and Dothan 1971; Perlman and Asaro 1982; Gunneweg *et al.* 1986: Table 1).
2. Other examples of the work of relocated potters may be 'imitation' Cypriote Bichrome Ware of the LBI period which is indistinguishable from Cypriote Bichrome Ware except that it was made in Canaan (Wood 1982), and the application of a Mesopotamian decoration to Iron II bowls (Zertal 1989).

Village potters in Spain are often required to relocate because of economic pressures. Many of the potters of Salvatierra de los Barros left the town and established workshops in other communities within a 200 km radius (Vossen 1984:346). Similarly, extreme competition fostered by middlemen forced a number of the potters of Agost to emigrate, some as far away as the Canary Islands and Puerto Rico (1984:359). In the example of Bé cited above, there is a great deal of movement of potters as a result of marriage, emigration and visitation (David and Hennig 1972:4-6, 21-22).

Spatial Style Variability
Pottery styles are much like modern automobile styles. There is a great similarity between contemporary examples of a given automobile model, even though they are manufactured in production centers far removed from one another. Yet there are distinguishing features that enable the discerning eye to differentiate the product of one company from that of another. The same is true in pottery styles. Although pottery vessels are produced according to a particular 'mental template' at a given point in time, and there is a general uniformity in ceramic style across Palestine, minor variations frequently exist between the work of different workshops or regions. This may be due to raw materials, culture, or outside influences.

In Guatemala, for example, pottery forms

> can be divided into five major groups according to function...
> and each pottery-production center has its own variants of these
> forms... Vessels do not generally travel far or sell well outside
> their region. Here the style of specific vessels (body shape, han-
> dle placement, etc.) are too well established culturally through
> the concept of *costumbre* [the 'law of the saints'] (Reina and Hill
> 1978:24-25, 216, 219; cf. London 1987b).

Such regional variation can be observed in the pottery of ancient Palestine as, for example, in the cooking pot of the Late Bronze–Iron Age transitional period (Wood 1985: 388-96).

Superimposed on this macrovariation is microvariation. No two vessels are precisely identical in all of their attributes even though they may be made in the same production center.

Since potters are humans and not machines, small variations exist between the work of different potters, or in the work of any one potter (Clarke 1978:178; Rice 1981:220). Impey and Pollard have used multivariate analysis to differentiate the work of three different potters whose work was indistinguishable to the naked eye (1985). Many potters claim that they can identify their work, and the work of other potters, by these variations (Foster 1965:45; Matson 1972:221; Stanislawski 1978:215; Nicholson and Patterson 1985b:234).

Hill (1977) has investigated the differences between the work of individuals, with the goal of identifying the products of particular artisans in the archaeological record. Five subjects were asked to make twenty exact copies of a simple design element using the same brush. It was found that individual variation in motor performance is unavoidable and probably subconscious. And yet, each individual's performances departed from the template in different and regular ways (1977:61). Hill also investigated hand-writing analysis and found that the amount of change in an individual's motor performance with age is insufficient to prevent the identification of the work of an individual (1977:92).

Temporal Variability of Ceramic Style

In addition to the macrovariation of style through space (regional variation), there is macrovariation of style through time. As with the automobile, pottery styles, particularly morphological features, change gradually with time.[1] This phenomenon is the basis for ceramic chronology (Shepard 1956:341-48; James 1962:37; Lapp 1975:36).

In general, potters are conservative and do not readily make changes in their routine (Voyatzoglou 1974:24; Franken 1982:142; Arnold 1985:229; Kramer 1985:92, 96; Nicholson and Patterson 1985b:237). Foster gave considerable attention to this aspect of the ceramic industry in Tzintzuntzan. He found the potters less likely to be innovators than their non-potting contemporaries, which seems to be true of potters everywhere (1965:49). The reason for this, Foster believes, is

1. For theoretical considerations, see Binford 1965:205-208; Hill 1985.

that potters tend to continue tried and proven fabrication techniques in order to minimize the risk of failure (1965:49; cf. Arnold 1985:229).

Because of this inherent conservatism, sudden changes in the ceramic repertoire are probably due to foreign intrusion (Franken 1982:142). Examples of such intrusion in Palestine are MB IIA ware and Philistine ware. The reappearance of older types may also account for such changes, as suggested by Dever (1970:20).

Factors Affecting Temporal Style Change
The gradual morphological changes that occur through time are due to slight variations resulting from multiple replications of an object formed from a plastic medium.[1] Because of the intense interaction previously discussed, these slight variations become the norm and the same morphological changes are observed over a wide area.

Certain vessels change more rapidly than others. The cooking pot, for example, changes very rapidly in the Bronze and Iron Age and is an excellent chronological indicator. Such rapid change is undoubtedly related to production volume (Lance 1981:43). Cooking pots received daily harsh usage and since they were in the center of domestic activity were highly vulnerable. As a result, the life span of a cooking pot was much shorter than that of other vessels (see below). The potter, then, was called upon to fabricate many more cooking pots than other vessels, giving rise to a comparatively rapid morphological change.

Hodges conducted an experiment using students to illustrate this principle. An original pot was copied by one student. The original was removed and the copy reproduced by two other students, independently. The first copy was then removed and reproductions were made of the second copies, and so on, to provide two sequences of five copies each. The results are quite illuminating (fig. 24); the fifth copy in each sequence degenerated significantly from the original prototype. With repeated copying, the vessel became shorter, the rim became more

1. For an interesting example of style change in a nonplastic medium, see Cleland 1972.

everted, and a distinct base appeared. The same was true of both sequences.

This is perhaps an exaggerated example, since the work was done by inexperienced students using the coil-built method. With experienced potters using a wheel, changes would not be as dramatic, but changes would occur nonetheless. And the tendency towards degeneration is exactly what is observed in the archaeological record: when a new type is introduced into the ceramic repertoire and replication begins, the new type degenerates with time. These results suggest the possibility that, through the operation of human factors inherent in the act of making pottery, similar degenerative changes may have been taking place simultaneously in different areas of the country (Franken 1982:142).[1]

A Proposed Model for the Temporal Variability of Ceramic Style

It has been noted that ceramic morphology changes with time and this morphological variation allows the ceramic typologist to date pottery within a fairly narrow time range, usually 25–50 years. It has also been noted that morphological changes seem to occur simultaneously and at the same rate all across Palestine. A hypothesis which explains this phenomenon is comprised of three postulates based on the above observations:

Postulate 1   Ceramic morphological variability is primarily degenerative in nature.

Postulate 2   Ceramic morphological variability is related to factors inherent in the production process and is therefore proportional to the rate of production.

1. These factors may have included the motor characteristics of the potters, efforts to take short cuts, etc. J.S. Holladay, Jr, suggests that a similar element may have been present in the production process itself. While a freshly turned vessel is drying to a leather-hard state, it tends to sag slightly. This sag, coupled with repeated replication, results in a vessel that becomes squatter with time (personal communication). Since the same production procedures were in use throughout the country, degenerative factors inherent in the process would be common to all production centers and would thus tend to maintain the uniformity of shape, even though it was changing with time.

Postulate 3   Since ceramic morphological variability is
related to factors inherent in the production
process, the same morphological variability
will occur simultaneously in all locations
where similar production is taking place.
Minor differences between localities due to
rate of production, potters' skill, raw materials,
etc., will tend to harmonize over a large area as
a result of the various factors which contribute
to the diffusion of ceramic style.

In order to test this hypothesis, it would be necessary to
observe an operating potters' workshop over a long period of
time, perhaps several decades.[1] Samples of the same vessel
type would have to be taken periodically and compared with
past samples. In addition, other data such as production volume, potter's skill, and so on, would have to be recorded.

Vessel Lifespan

Once pottery reaches the place of its intended use, the consumer's home, a number of questions come to mind. How was
pottery used? That is to say, what utilitarian function did it
perform? What was the customer's attitude toward the pottery? What was an average household assemblage? What
were the lifespans of various types of vessels? We shall attempt
to answer these questions by appealing to ethnographic observations.

Pottery and the Customer

The potter will obviously produce only those items that can be
sold and which will bring a profit. Production, therefore, is
based on customer demand. The customer, on the other hand,
will buy only those vessels which fulfill functional needs and
are culturally acceptable. In Guatemala, Reina and Hill found

1. Another way to test this hypothesis is through experimentation
(Binford 1983:24, 104). It is doubtful, however, that it would be possible
to duplicate all of the conditions present in an actual operating potters'
shop, such as day-in, day-out volume production over an extended
period of time, economic pressures, etc.

that pottery is intimately related to a traditional diet and to specific ways of preparing food, as well as to custom. The association between diet and pottery is inseparable and changes do not occur easily (1978:209). Merchants handle only those items that they know will sell; over the years, they have learned the requirements of the conservative local customer.

> Although many pottery vessels look alike to an outsider, they are distinctive in appearance from the user's point of view... It is socially desirable to keep *costumbre*; for this a wide assortment of vessels for storing food and water, for cooking different types of food, and for serving is necessary. Women have a great interest in utensils. During a market day, they like to admire vessels by tapping them, judging their quality, and looking at them from an aesthetic point of view. When a good vessel meets with *costumbre*, bargaining becomes aggressive, and the consumer tries as quickly as possible to reach an agreeable price. Such vessels sell rapidly, while inferior objects are left for harder bargaining. But these too are part of *costumbre*, and an individual with less money, in urgent need of a cooking or storage vessel, will feel satisfied that she too complies with *costumbre* on a more humble level (1978:238, 248).

In Darfur, Sudan, there are three types of cooking pots: one for milk, one for meat and one for porridge, the only difference being in size. There are two water pots, a small one for carrying and a large one for storing water. Three pots, with the only difference being in size, are associated with beer: one for brewing, one for serving, and one for storing (Haaland 1978:56). The Kalinga natives in the northern Philippines classify their cooking pots according to two types: those for rice and those for meat and vegetables. These types occur in three sizes: small, medium and very large. Water jars form another type (Longacre 1985:337). Thus, particular vessels serve particular functions in the mind of the customer.[1]

---

1. See also Okpoko 1987:450-52. For discussions of the correlation between morphological attributes and vessel use, see Henrickson and McDonald 1983; M. Smith 1985; Rice 1987:207-43. On the relationship between vessel content and function, see Cackette, D'Auria and Snow 1987. For studies on the function of pottery in ancient Palestine, see Honeyman 1939: Sukenik 1940; Kelso 1948:11-32; Amiran and Dothan 1952; James 1962; 1966:28; R.H. Smith 1964; Kaplan 1965; 1972:73;

Typical Household Assemblages

Although one would expect that the number of vessels present in a household would vary in proportion to the size of the household, several ethnographic studies indicate that this is not the case. It appears that the number of vessels owned by a family unit is more closely related to status and wealth (Kramer 1985:91-92; Longacre 1985:337). The data collected by Tschopik from the village of Chucuito, Peru, reflect this fact (table 2).

Another important factor influencing the ceramic population is the use of non-ceramic containers. Among the Huichol, an aboriginal group in Mexico, gourds are used extensively for drawing, transporting and storing water and are used more often than pottery for serving food (Weigand 1969:17, 20). As a result, the number of ceramic vessels in a typical household is minimal (1969: table III). The minimum number of pots per household is nine to ten in Darfur, Sudan. There, wood, skin, gourd or, mostly, basketry containers are used in addition to pottery (Haaland 1978:56, 57). This stands in sharp contrast to 50–75 ceramic vessels per household in Tzintzuntzan, Mexico, in 1959 when pottery was the prevailing receptacle for carrying and storing water, and for cooking, eating and drinking (Foster 1960:607, 608). In 1970 Reina and Hill observed that the average kitchen inventory in Guatemala was nineteen vessels. Eighteen of those vessels cost a total of $4.94, while one large water storage vessel cost $2.20 (1978:246).

The use of metal and plastic containers is now affecting nearly all studies on vessel frequencies (David and Hennig 1972:21; Kramer 1985:91; Longacre 1985:345). Data on household ceramic inventories gleaned from several ethnographic studies are presented in table 3.

Leonard 1981; Rainey 1982. On the Egyptian amphora, see Wood 1987. On Mesopotamian vessels, see Ellison 1984.

Lifespan of Household Pottery[1]

Foster made a detailed study of the lifespan of household pottery vessels in Tzintzuntzan, Mexico. He observed five factors which affect their life expectancy (1960:608; cf. Arnold 1985:152-55).[2]

1. Basic strength—Life varies directly with the hardness of the ware.
2. Vessel use—Cooking pots which are used daily have the shortest lifespan. Casseroles, plates and cups, also in daily use, last a little longer. Large water jars, although intrinsically weaker, are placed in a protected position and therefore have a long life. Large fiesta pots and casseroles have the longest life because they are thick and strong and are used only a few times a year.
3. Mode of use—Objects used at waist height last longer than those used at or near ground level.
4. Breakage agents—The presence of animals, children or a careless user increases the risk of vessel breakage.
5. Pottery costs—More expensive vessels are given greater care and therefore last longer.

Most Mexican vessels are glazed, which provides additional strength over that of unglazed ware (Foster 1960:608). Foster found that the average life of cooking and eating vessels was one year; water jars last a little longer and festive cooking wares last the longest (1960:608). He noted a water jar that was 22 years old and an enormous vessel with a capacity of 45 litres that was 40–50 years old (1960:607). Vossen found that water pitchers last about two years in Spain (1984: 343).

The women of Guatemala take especially good care of their pottery. For them, it is socially prestigious to own pottery

1. For overviews of studies on the longevity of ceramic vessels, see Kramer 1985:89-91; Longacre 1985: 334-36; Arnold 1985:152-55.
2. It should be noted that vessels found in a cultic context are not subjected to factors 2, 3, and 4. One would normally expect, therefore, that vessels found in a temple would be of a greater age than those found in a contemporary dwelling. For an example of this phenomenon, see Brug 1985:76, 107. Okpoko found that ritual vessels kept in shrines in eastern Nigeria had an estimated lifespan of 50 years and above, whereas the same types of vessels in domestic use had an estimated lifespan of one year or less (1987:453).

which has been handed down for several generations (Reina
and Hill 1978:246). Reina and Hill were shown one large vessel that had been made at the beginning of the century (1978:
pl. 407). Similarly, a large cooking pot being used by the
aboriginal Huichol in Mexico was estimated to be 70 years old
(Weigand 1969:33). London observed large pithoi on the island
of Cyprus that were well over a century old (1989:44).

In general, ethnographic studies show that vessel lifespan is
related to vessel size: the larger the vessel, the longer it lasts.
This maxim seems to be related to vessel mobility and cost. In
1971 DeBoer studied the pottery habits of the Conibo, a
hunter-gatherer culture in Peru. He collected data from
seven nuclear families made up of 34 individuals. On the basis
of vessel lifespan, DeBoer projected that the number of vessels
being discarded by these families was 206 in one year, 546 in 5
years and 2248 in 25 years (1974:338).

Ceramic longevity data collected by ethnographers, summarized here in table 4, indicate that ordinary household vessels in daily use will last no more than a few years, but large
vessels which are given special care, or vessels used only infre-
quently, or that have intrinsic value, may last several decades
or longer. Another factor that must be taken into account
when pottery is used for dating purposes is that broken vessels
are often used secondarily for a considerable length of time
(Stanislawski 1969; DeBoer and Lathrap 1979: table 4.4;
Kramer 1985:89; Okpoko 1987:453).

Summary and Conclusions

From archaeological findings, it is evident that similar
ceramic styles were widely dispersed in ancient Palestine.
Archaeological, literary and ethnographic data suggest that a
number of circumstances were responsible for this phenomenon: commercial sale of vessels, commercial container traffic,
state container traffic, relocating consumers, itinerant potters
and relocating potters. The most prominent of these was no
doubt the commercial sale of pottery. Ordinary domestic
wares were rapidly diffused throughout the country from
urban production centers by itinerant merchants who sold

their wares through the existing market system and independently from village to village.

As a result of factors inherent in the production process, ceramic styles degenerated with time in proportion to production volume. Since the production process was generally consistent across the country, and because of the factors that produced a uniformity of style, temporal style changes were much the same in different parts of the country.

The consumer undoubtedly placed a high value on cooking and eating vessels, expecting them to be functional, as well as meeting stylistic requirements. Vessels in daily use would last only a few years, while larger vessels, special-use vessels, and vessels with high intrinsic value, were given greater care and would last, perhaps several decades, or even longer.

With the above information in mind, we can now intelligently address the questions raised earlier concerning time lag in the spread of ceramic style. Relative to Kenyon's statement on the contemporaneity of vessels of similar form and the 'almost contemporary spread of newly introduced types', we may say that her observation is entirely correct. Due to the rapid diffusion of pottery vessels by merchants, the intense interaction between potters and pottery, and the limited lifespan of most utilitarian vessels, the time lag between the initial fabrication of a vessel and its final deposition in the archaeological record was very short, only a few years.

A time increment of several years is insignificant in comparison with the observable macrovariation in temporal style change which is of the order of decades or centuries. From the point of view of the archaeologist, therefore, if a chronologically diagnostic vessel of the same form is found at two different sites, the two vessels can be considered to be contemporary. Caution must be exercised, however, with regard to large vessels or vessels which have a high intrinsic value. They may have lifespans of decades, or even longer in the case of heirlooms. The same note of caution must be sounded relative to vessels found in cultic contexts. Such vessels were not subjected to the same conditions as their household counterparts and therefore tended to have much longer lifespans.

The question which Franken raises with regard to the possibility that pottery styles of a small village may lag behind those of a large urban center need not be a matter of concern. The pottery merchant traveled to the smallest village or hamlet; he took his wares to any location where he could turn a profit. If imported vessels made their way to a small site such as Deir 'Allā (Hankey 1981:113-15), certainly the same merchants would have brought local wares from urban production centers as well. Several of the other factors at work in the diffusion of ceramic style, such as commercial container traffic, relocating consumers and possibly itinerant potters, were present in the small village as well as in the urban center.

On the matter of the work of Deetz and Dethlefsen on American grave stone styles and its relevance to the pottery styles of ancient Palestine, it can be emphatically stated that a motif which has significant religious and cultural overtones, produced in a non-plastic medium by a small number of artisans, has no bearing whatsoever on pottery styles in ancient Palestine.[1] The style of a utilitarian vessel mass-produced in a plastic medium by a large number of workers at many locations follows an entirely different set of determinants and the two simply cannot be compared.

On the basis of the evidence considered in this survey, we can confidently conclude that a study of the continuous and subtle changes in vessel morphology as determined from stratified deposits, combined with comparative analyses of material from other sites, remains the most effective chronological tool available to the Palestinian archaeologist.

1. Subsequent work by other investigators has shown that colonial grave stone motifs do not follow the ideal pattern of lenticular popularity envisioned by Deetz and Dethlefsen. The popularity of these designs can be affected by a number of non-chronological factors such as local variations in style, local preferences by craftsmen and their products, and the isolation of some rural communities from the mainstream styles (Baugher and Winter 1983:48). Such factors radically affect the spatial diffusion of grave stone motifs as well.

TABLES AND FIGURES

The Sociology of Pottery

Table 1
Provenience of Palestinian Domestic Wares
from Tel el-Hesi and Gezer

Site	Locally Made	Made in the Coastal Plain [a]	Made in the Jerusalem Area
Tell el-Hesi [b]	38%	53%	9%
Gezer [c]	44%	28%	3%

Note: Data obtained from Brooks *et al.* 1974:64-73.
a. It was not possible to pinpoint exact sources for pottery in this category (1974:72).
b. Based on a sample of 225 sherds.
c. Based on a sample of 32 sherds. Eight of the sherds (25%) were of unknown provenience (1974:64).

Table 2
Household Assemblages for Four Families
in Chucuito, Peru, 1940–1942

| Vessel | Economic Status | | | |
	Wealthy	Middle Class	Poor	Poor
Cooking Pot	14	11	7	8
Jug	11	2	2	2
Toasting Vessel	5	3	1	2
Basin	7	7	2	3
Large Store Jar	5	1	2	0
Bowl	45	19	17	12
Cup	13	5	0	0
Stove	4	2	1	1
Pottery Lamp	0	0	0	1
Incense Burner	2	0	1	0
Figurine	9	5	1	0
Glazed Piece	5	2	2	1
Metal Candlestick	7	4	0	0
Wooden Bowl	2	2	2	0
Kerosene Lamp	3	1	0	0
Enamel Basin	6	4	0	0
Enamel Pitcher	2	3	0	0
Wooden Barrel	3	0	0	0
Gasoline Tin	8	3	3	1
Bottle	0	8	0	2
Tin Cup	0	0	3	0
Tin Oil Lamp	0	0	1	0

Note: Data obtained from Tschopik 1950:215-16; household size not stated

Table 3

Average Ceramic Inventory for Typical Households in Various Cultures

Location

Type of Culture	Bé, North Cameroon [a] Tribal Village	Luzon, the Philippines				Ucayli River Forest, Peru [d] Hunter-Gatherer
		Dangtalan [b] Tribal Village		Dalupa [c] Tribal Village		
Time of Survey	1970	1975-76	1979-80	1975-76	1979-80	1971
Number of Households	15	49	49	44	44	18
Vessel						
Small Cooking Pot	4.3	—	—	—	—	0.8
Medium Cooking Pot	7.7	5.1	6.2e	3.1	5.8e	1.7
Large Cooking Pot	2.3	1.9	5.4e	0.4	0.7e	1.2
Bowl	2.2	—	—	—	—	3.4
Mug	—	—	—	—	—	1.2
Small Jar	—	—	—	—	—	0.8
Medium Jar	—	1.8	1.1f	2.0	2.0	2.0
Large Jar	3.1	—	—	—	—	0.8
Miscellaneous	1.3	0.9	0.7	0.1	0.3	1.3
Total	20.9	9.7	13.4	5.6	8.8	13.2

a. David and Hennig 1972:17.
b. Longacre 1985: table 13.2.
c. Longacre 1985: table 13.3.
d. DeBoer and Lathrap 1979: table 4.3.
e. The increase in cooking pots between 1976 and 1980 in Dangtalan and Dalupa was due to an improved economic situation (Longacre 1985:341-45).
f. The decrease in medium (water) jars between 1976 and 1980 in Dangtalan was due to an increase in plastic water containers made possible by an improved economic situation (Longacre 1985:345).

Table 4

Mean Vessel Lifespan for Different Vessel Types in Various Cultures, in Years

Type of Culture	Bé, North Cameroon[a] Tribal Village	Tzintzuntzan, Mexico[b] Urban Village	Luzon, the Philippines[c] Dangtalan Tribal Village	Dalupa Tribal Village	Ucayli River Forest, Peru[d] Hunter-Gatherer
Number of Households	15	4	49	44	18
Vessel					
Small Cooking Pot	2.7	1	—	—	1.13
Medium Cooking Pot	2.5	1	4.65/4.23e	5.45/3.54e	0.88
Large Cooking Pot	10.2	1	13.80/13.00e	9.00/—e	1.38
Bowl	2.7	1	—	—	0.31
Mug	—	1	—	—	0.24
Jug	—	>1	—	—	—
Small Jar	—	>1	—	—	0.71
Medium Jar	—	>1	—	—	0.78
Large Jar	12.5	>1	8.17	7.18	1.13
Exceptional Cases	Three large store jars >130 years old	Water jar 22 years old enormous vessel 40–50 years old	—	—	—

a. David and Hennig 1972:21-22; cf. Bedaux and van der Waals 1987.

b. Foster 1960:607-608.

c. Longacre 1985: table 13.1.

d. DeBoer and Lathrap 1979: table 4.5.

e. Rice cooking pot and vegetable/meat cooking pot, respectively.

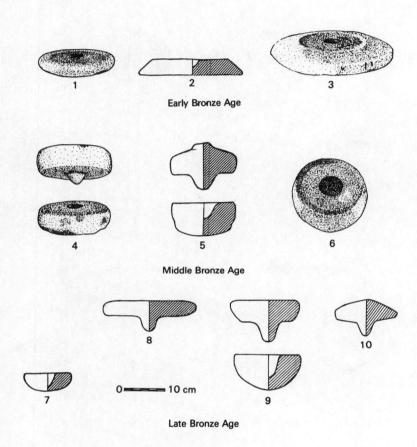

Figure 1. Potter's wheel thrust bearings from the Bronze Age, all of basalt. 1. Megiddo Str. XVIII, after Loud 1948: pl. 268.1; 2. Jericho H.xiii-xiv, after Kenyon and Holland 1983: fig. 231.2; 3. Megiddo Str. XVI, after Loud 1948: pl. 268:2; 4. Megiddo XV, after Loud 1948: pl. 268.3; 5. Jericho City C, after Garstang 1934: pl. 19.2; 6. Lachish Grid Square A.26, after Tufnell *et al.* 1958: pl. 21.1; 7. Sarepta Sounding Y Str. K, after Anderson 1979: pl. 22.10; 8. Hazor Str. 1B, after Yadin *et al.* 1958: pl. 87.24; 9, 10. Hazor Str. 1B, Yadin *et al.* 1960: pl. 127.22, 23.

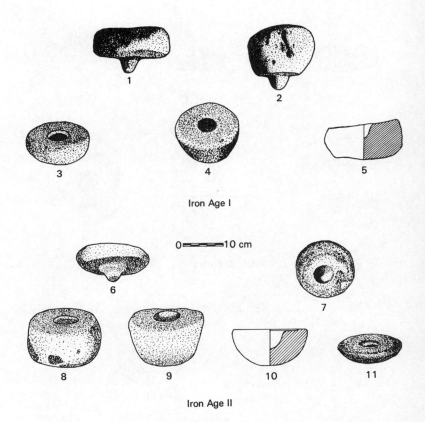

Iron Age I

0 ▭▬▬▬ 10 cm

Iron Age II

Figure 2. Potter's wheel thrust bearings from the Iron Age, all of basalt except no. 2 which is of limestone. 1, 2. Lachish Cave 4034, after Tufnell *et al.* 1958: pl. 49.12, 13; 3. Gezer Field VI Str. 5A-C, after Dever *et al.* 1971: fig. 15d; 4. Megiddo Str. V, after Lamon and Shipton 1939: pl. 114.2; 5. Hazor Str. IX, Yadin *et al.* 1961: pl. 213.15; 6. Megiddo Cave 4, after Guy 1938: pl. 153.11; 7. Megiddo Str. II, after Lamon and Shipton 1939: pl. 114.3; 8. Megiddo Cave 59, after Guy 1938: pl. 157.17; 9. Megiddo Cave 26, after Guy 1938: pl. 154.13; 10. Hazor Str. III, Yadin *et al.* 1958: pl. 77.18; 11. Megiddo Str. II, after Lamon and Shipton 1939: pl. 114.1.

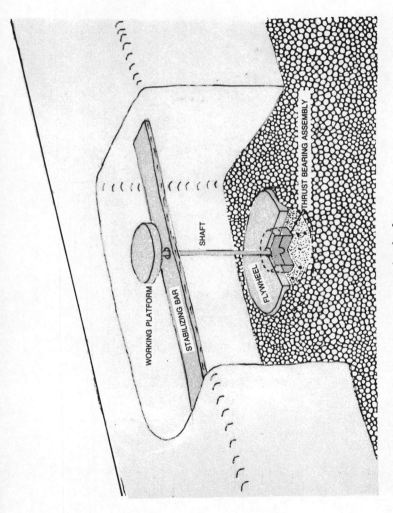

Figure 3. Reconstruction of a double potter's wheel.

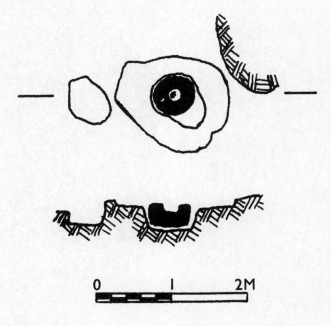

Figure 4. Plan and section of the potter's wheel emplacement in Cave 37 at Megiddo (Guy 1938: fig. 84.H).

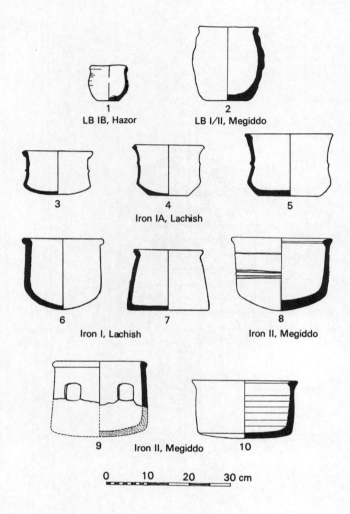

Figure 5. Potters' jars from the Late Bronze and Iron Ages: 1. Yadin *et al.* 1961: pl. 269.21; 2. Guy 1938: pl. 37.12; 3-5. Tufnell *et al.* 1958: pl. 79.808, 809, 811; 6, 7. Tufnell 1953: pl. 90.393, 394; 8-10. Guy 1938: pls. 38.29, 30; 39.2.

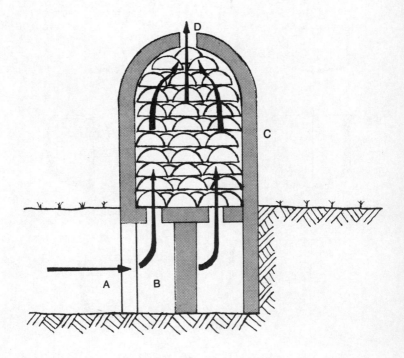

Figure 6. Schematic cross-section of a vertical (updraft) kiln: A—stoking pit, B—fire box, C—pottery chamber, D—exit flue.

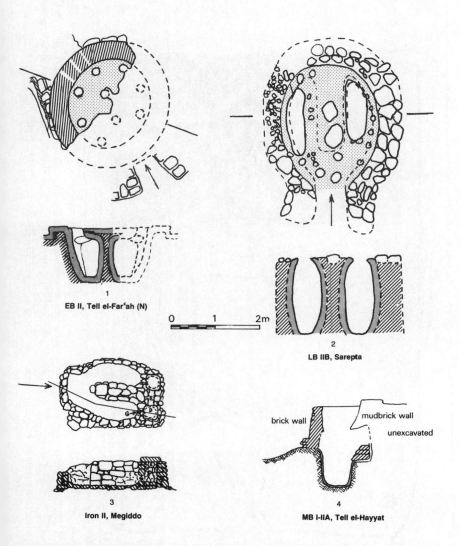

Figure 7. Vertical kilns from the Bronze and Iron Ages. 1. De Vaux 1955: fig. 9; 2. Pritchard 1975: fig. 14; 3. Guy 1938: fig. 89; 4. Falconer, Magness-Gardiner and Metzger 1984: fig. 4.

Figure 8. Pinax fragment (right) and conjectured restoration (left) showing a schematic drawing of the interior of a Greek vertical kiln. Vases are shown inside the pottery chamber, which is isolated from the fire box by a perforated floor. The floor is supported by a column. Burning embers in the fire-box are represented by dots in the lower left hand corner of the scene. At the top of the kiln is an exit flue. Near the flue are two small test pieces, with hook holes, to be removed during the course of firing to test kiln conditions (Noble 1965:73-74, fig. 238).

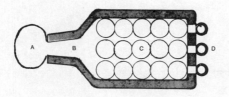

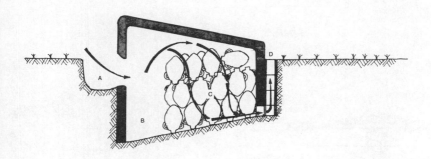

Figure 9. Schematic cross-section of a horizontal (downdraft) kiln: A—stoking pit, B—fire box, C—pottery chamber, D—exit flue.

108

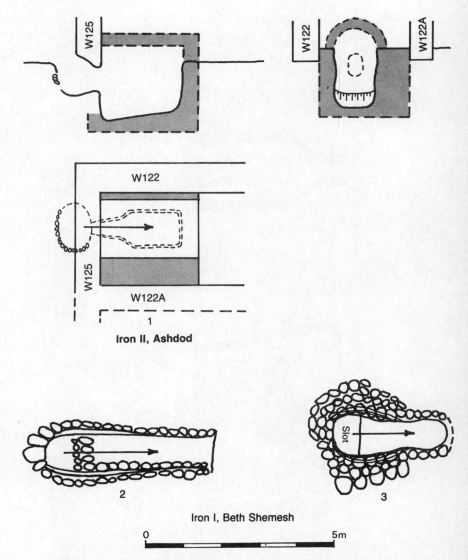

Figure 10. Horizontal kilns from the Iron Age. 1. M. Dothan 1971: plan 12.1088; 2. Grant 1934: map III.490; 3. Grant 1934: map II.441. Nos. 2 and 3 reproduced courtesy of the Treasure Room, Haverford College Library, Haverford, PA.

Figure 11. Eighteenth Dynasty tomb painting showing all of the essential elements of a pottery workshop. The master potter sits at a single wheel fashioning a vessel from a conical lump of clay. An assistant turns the wheel and aids the potter with the clay. Behind the potter are rows of vessels, probably newly formed and in the process of air drying. In the foreground another assistant kneads clay with his feet, preparing it for the master potter. To his left are two large jars, undoubtedly containing water to be mixed with the clay. In the background are two baskets containing a reddish material, possibly prepared clay, and a pile of the same material on the floor. To the right of the scene a worker seals the top of a vertical kiln, probably in preparation for firing. Tomb of Kenamun, Thebes (Davies 1930: pl. 59).

110

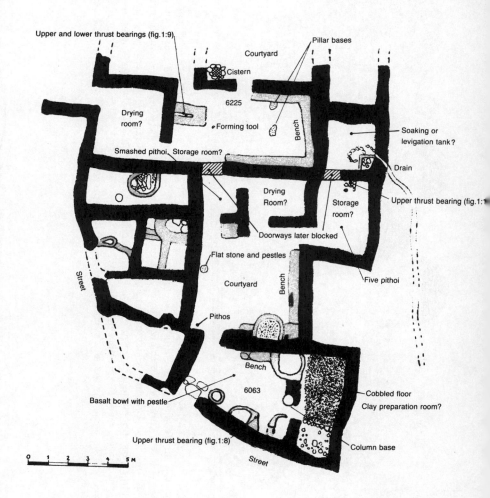

Figure 12. LB IIA pottery workshops associated with the Stelae Shrine, Hazor Area C, Str. 1B (after Yadin *et al.* 1960: pl. 208).

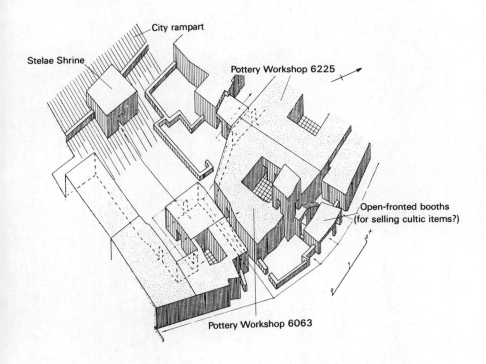

Figure 13. Isometric reconstruction of Hazor Stelae Shrine and associated buildings (Yadin *et al.* 1960: fig. 5).

112

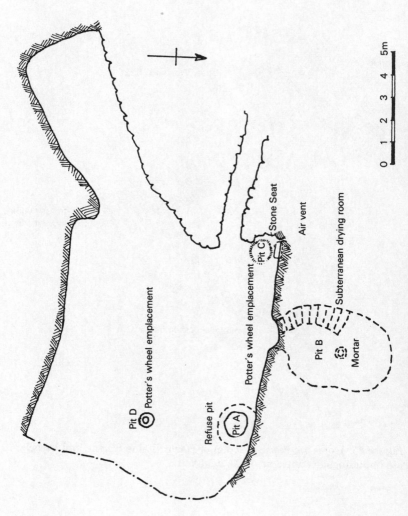

Figure 14. Potters' Cave 4034 at Lachish (after Tufnell *et al.* 1958: pl. 92).

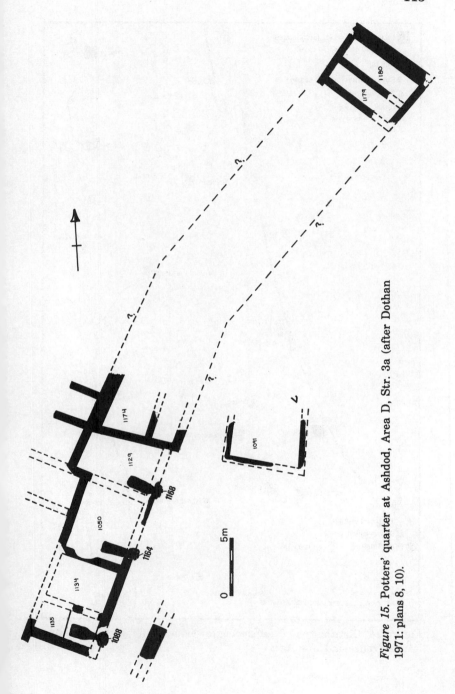

Figure 15. Potters' quarter at Ashdod, Area D, Str. 3a (after Dothan 1971: plans 8, 10).

114

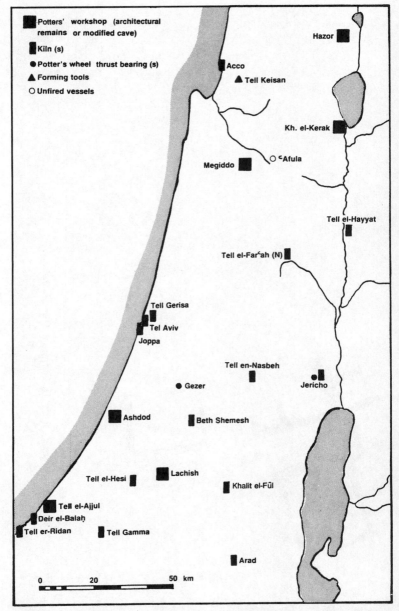

Figure 16. Distribution of archaeological evidence for pottery making in the Bronze and Iron Ages.

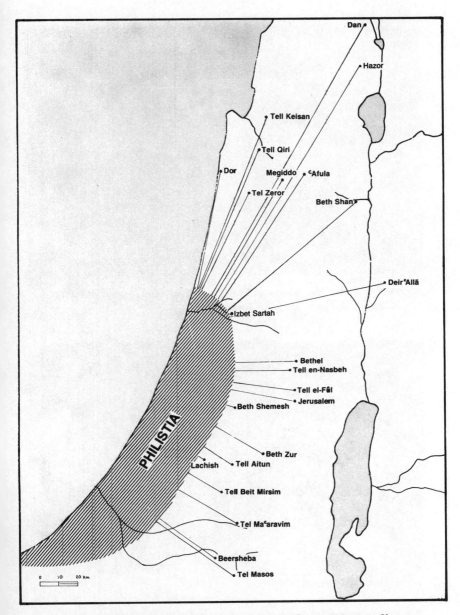

Figure 17. Distribution of Philistine Ware (after Dothan 1982: map 2).

116

Figure 18. Water jars, bowls and braziers being transported by donkey, Casablanca, Morocco (phot. R. Vossen, 1980).

Figure 19. Pottery for sale in a market at Gueddara, Morocco (phot. W. Ebert, 1980).

Figure 20. Pottery merchants in Guatemala setting out with their wares (phot. Rubin E. Reina; Pl. 382 of *The Traditional Pottery of Guatemala* by R.E. Reina and R.M. Hill II, University of Texas Press, 1978).

118

Figure 21. Pottery for sale in a market at Bine el-Qidane, Morocco
(phot. R. Vossen, 1980).

Figure 22. Water jars being transported by cart, Sidi Rahal, Morocco (phot. R. Vossen, 1980).

120

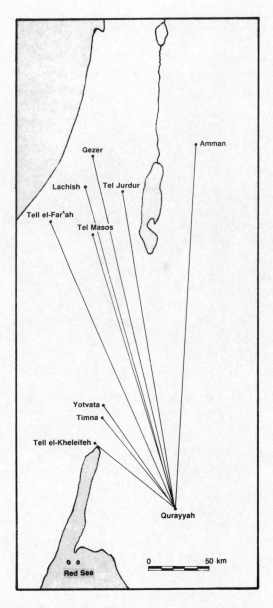

Figure 23. Distribution of 'Midianite ware' (after Kalsbeek and London 1978: fig. 1; with the addition of Gezer, Brandl 1984).

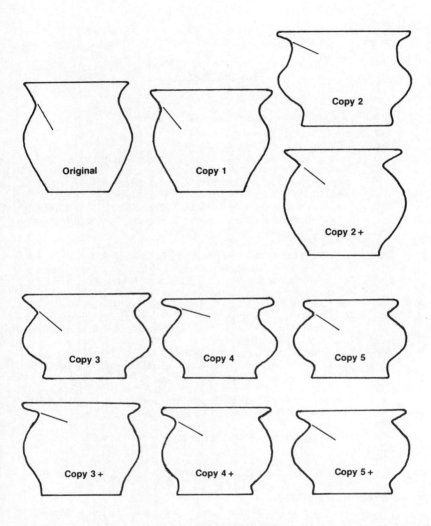

Figure 24. Degeneration of ceramic form with repeated replication (Hodges 1965: fig. 3). Reprinted from *Ceramics and Man*, ed. F.R. Matson, Viking Fund Publications in Anthropology, 41, 1965, by permission of the Wenner-Gren Foundation for Anthropological Research, New York.

BIBLIOGRAPHY

Aharoni, Y.
1967   'Arad'. *Israel Exploration Journal* 17:270-72.
1968   'Tel Arad'. *Revue Biblique* 75:389-92.
1975   *Investigations at Lachish: The Sanctuary and the Residency (Lachish 5)*. Tel Aviv: Tel Aviv University Institute of Archaeology.
1979   *Land of the Bible: A Historical Geography*. Rev. edn, trans. from 1962 Hebrew edn by A.F. Rainey. Philadelphia: Westminster.
1982   *The Archaeology of the Land of Israel*. Ed. Miriam Aharoni; trans. from 1978 Hebrew edn by A.F. Rainey. Philadelphia: Westminster.
Albright, W.F.
1932   *The Excavation of Tell Beit Mirsim in Palestine*, vol. 1. *The Pottery of the First Three Campaigns*. Annual of the American Schools of Oriental Research, 12 for 1930–1931. Cambridge, MA: American Schools of Oriental Research.
1933   *The Excavation of Tell Beit Mirsim*, vol. 1A. *The Pottery of the Fourth Campaign*. Pp. 55-127 in Annual of the American Schools of Oriental Research, 13 for 1931–1932. Cambridge, MA: American Schools of Oriental Research.
1938   *The Excavation of Tell Beit Mirsim*, vol. 2. *The Bronze Age*. Annual of the American Schools of Oriental Research, 17 for 1936–1937. Cambridge, MA: American Schools of Oriental Research.
1943   *The Excavation of Tell Beit Mirsim*, vol. 3. *The Iron Age*. Annual of the American Schools of Oriental Research, 21-22 for 1941–1943. Cambridge, MA: American Schools of Oriental Research.
Alezadeh, A.
1985   'A Protoliterate Kiln from Chogha Mish'. *Iran* 23:39-50.
Amiran, R.
1969   *Ancient Pottery of the Holy Land: From its Beginnings in the Neolithic Period to the End of the Iron Age*. Trans. from the 1963 Hebrew edn. Jerusalem: Masada.
Amiran, R., and M. Dothan
1952   'Two Notes on the "Double Bowl"'. *Bulletin of the Israel Exploration Society* 17:144-52 (Hebrew).
Amiran, R., and J. Glass
1979   'An Archaeological Petrographical Study of 15 W-Ware Pots in the Ashmolean Museum'. *Tel Aviv* 6:54-59.
Amiran, R., and D. Shenhav
1984   'Experiments With an Ancient Potter's Wheel'. Pp. 107-12 in *Pots and Potters: Current Approaches in Ceramic Archaeology*. Ed. P.M. Rice. University of California Institute of Archaeology Monograph, 24. Los Angeles: University of California.

Amiran (Kallner), R., and J. Vroman
1946   'Petrographic Examination of Pottery'. *Bulletin of the Jewish Palestine Exploration Society* 12:10-15 (Hebrew, English summary p. i).

Anderson, W.P.
1975   'The Stratigraphy of Sounding Y'. Pp. 41-52 in *Sarepta: A Preliminary Report on the Iron Age*, by J.B. Pritchard. Philadelphia: The University Museum.
1979   'A Stratigraphic and Ceramic Analysis of the Late Bronze and Iron Age Strata of Sounding Y at Sarepta (Sarafand, Lebanon)'. Ph.D. dissertation, University of Pennsylvania. Ann Arbor, MI: University Microfilms International.

Annis, M.B., and H. Geertman
1987   'Production and Distribution of Cooking Ware in Sardinia'. *Newsletter, Department of Pottery Technology, University of Leiden* 5:154-96.

Arnold, D.E.
1972   'Native Pottery Making in Quinua', Peru'. *Anthropos* 67:858-72.
1978   'Ceramic Variability, Environment, and Culture History Among the Pokom in the Valley of Guatemala'. Pp. 39-60 in *The Spatial Organization of Culture*. Ed. I. Hodder. London: Duckworth.
1985   *Ceramic Theory and Cultural Process*. Cambridge: Cambridge University Press.

Asaro, F., I. Perlman and M. Dothan
1971   'An Introductory Study of Mycenaean IIIC1 Ware from Tel Ashdod'. *Archaeometry* 13:169-75.

Asboe, W.
1946   'Pottery in Ladakh, Western Tibet'. *Man* 46:9-10.

Åström, P. and R.E. Jones
1982   'A Mycenaean Tomb and its Near Eastern Connections'. *Opuscula Atheniensia* 14:7-9.

Badè, W.F.
1928   *Excavations at Tell En-Naṣbeh 1926 and 1927, a Preliminary Report*. Palestine Institute Publication, 1. Berkeley: Palestine Institute.

Balfet, H.
1965   'Ethnographic Observations in North Africa and Archaeological Interpretations: The Pottery of the Maghreb'. Pp. 161-77 in *Ceramics and Man*. Ed. F.R. Matson. Viking Fund Publications in Anthropology, 41. New York: Wenner-Gren Foundation for Anthropological Research.
1981   'Production and Distribution of Pottery in the Maghreb'. Pp. 257-69 in *Production and Distribution: A Ceramic Viewpoint*. Ed. H. Howard and E.L. Morris. BAR International Series, 120. Oxford: British Archaeological Reports.

Bankes, G.
1985   'The Manufacture and Circulation of Paddle and Anvil Pottery on the North Coast of Peru'. *World Archaeology* 17:269-77.

Barrelet, M.-T.
1968   *Figurines et reliefs en terre cuite de la Mésopotamie Antique 1: potiers, termes de métier, procédés de fabrication et production*. Paris: Librairie Orientaliste Paul Geuthner.

Baugher, S., and F.A. Winter
1983   'Early American Gravestones: Archaeological Perspectives on Three Cemeteries of Old New York'. *Archaeology* 36/5:46-53.

Beaudry, M.P.
1984   *Ceramic Production and Distribution in the Southeastern Maya Periphery: Late Classic Painted Serving Vessels*. BAR International Series, 203. Oxford: British Archaeological Reports.

Bedaux, R., and D. van der Waals
1987   'Aspects of Life-Span of Dogon Pottery'. *Newsletter, Department of Pottery Technology, University of Leiden* 5:137-53.

Bender, F.
1974   *Geology of Jordan*. Berlin: Gebrüder Bornträger.

Ben-Tor, A., and Y. Portugali
1987   'Tell Qiri, a Village in the Jezreel Valley; Report of the Archaeological Excavations 1975-1977'. *Qedem* 24. Jerusalem: Institute of Archaeology, Hebrew University.

Ben-Tor, A., Y. Portugali and M. Avissar
1981   'The First Two Seasons of Excavations at Tel Qashish 1978-1979: Preliminary Report'. *Israel Exploration Journal* 31:137-64.

Berry, B.J.L.
1967   *The Geography of Market Centers and Retail Distribution*. Englewood Cliffs, NJ: Prentice-Hall.

Bienkowski, P.
1986   *Jericho in the Late Bronze Age*. Warminster: Aris & Phillips.

Bikaki, A.H.
1984   *Keos 4, Ayia Irini: The Potter's Marks*. Mainz: Phillipp von Zabern.

Binford, L.R.
1965   'Archaeological Systematics and the Study of Culture Process'. *American Antiquity* 31:203-10.
1967   'Smudge Pits and Hide Smoking: The Use of Analogy in Archaeological Reasoning'. *American Antiquity* 32:1-12. Reprinted pp. 33-51 in *An Archaeological Perspective*, by L.R. Binford. New York: Seminar, 1972.
1983   *In Pursuit of the Past*. New York: Thames and Hudson.

Biran, A.
1974   'Tell er-Ruqeish to Tell er-Ridan'. *Israel Exploration Journal* 24:141-42.

Blackman, W.S.
1927   *The Fallahin of Upper Egypt*. London: Harrap.

Bliss, F.J.
1894   *A Mound of Many Cities*. London: Palestine Exploration Fund.

Bliss, F.J., and R.A.S. Macalister
1902   *Excavations in Palestine during the Years 1898-1900*. London: Palestine Exploration Fund.

Boardman, J.
1979   'The Athenian Pottery Trade: The Classical Period'. *Expedition* 21/4:33-39.

Borowski, O.
1988   'Ceramic Dating'. Pp. 223-33 in *Benchmarks in Time and Culture: An Introduction to Palestinian Archaeology*. Ed. J.F. Drinkard, Jr, G.L. Mattingly and J.M. Miller. American Schools of Oriental

Research and The Society of Biblical Literature Archaeology and Biblical Studies. Atlanta: Scholars.

Bourriau, J.
1981   *Umm el-Ga'ab: Pottery from the Nile Valley before the Arab Conquest.* Cambridge: Cambridge University Press.

Brandfon, F.R.
1981   'Norman Gottwald on the Tribes of Yahweh'. *Journal for the Study of the Old Testament* 21:101-10.

Brandl, B.
1984   'A Midianite Bowl from Gezer'. *Levant* 16:171-72.

Bresenham, M.J.
1985   'Descriptive and Experimental Study of Contemporary and Ancient Pottery Techniques at Buṣirā'. *Berytus* 33:89-101.

Briend, J., and H. Jean-Baptiste
1980   *Tell Keisan (1971-1976): Une cité phénicienne en Galilée.* Orbis Biblicus et Orientalis, Series Archaeologica, 1. Fribourg: Éditions Universitaires.

Brissaud, P.
1982   *Les Ateliers de potiers de la région de Louqsor.* Cairo: Institut Français d'Archéologie Orientale.

Brooks, D., A.M. Bieber, Jr, C. Harbottle, and E.V. Sayre
1974   'Biblical Studies through Activation Analysis of Ancient Pottery'. Pp. 48-80 in *Archaeological Chemistry.* Ed. C.W. Beck. Advances in Chemistry Series, 138. Washington, DC: American Chemical Society.

Brug, J.F.
1985   *A Literary and Archaeological Study of the Philistines.* BAR International Series, 265. Oxford: British Archaeological Reports.

Bullard, R.
1970   'Geological Studies in Field Archaeology'. *Biblical Archaeologist* 33:98-132.

Bunzel, R.L.
1929   *The Pueblo Potter, a Study of Creative Imagination in Primitive Art.* Reprint, New York: A.M.S., 1969.

Cackette, M., J.M. D'Auria, and B.E. Snow
1987   'Examining Earthenware Vessel Function by Elemental Phosphorus Content'. *Current Anthropology* 28:121-27.

Casson, S.
1938   'The Modern Pottery Trade in the Aegean'. *Antiquity* 12:464-73.
1951   'The Modern Pottery Trade in the Aegean: Further Notes'. *Antiquity* 25:187-90.

Charlton, T.H.
1976   'Modern Ceramics in the Teotihuacán Valley'. Pp. 137-48 in *Ethnic and Tourist Arts.* Ed. N.H.H. Graburn. Berkeley: University of California Press.

Charlton, T.H., and R.R. Katz
1979   'Tonalá Bruñida Ware Past and Present'. *Archaeology* 21/1:45-53.

Chazan, M., and P.E. McGovern
1984   'Kirbet Kerak Pottery at Beth Shan: Technological Evidence for Local Manufacture?' *MASCA Journal* 3:20-24.

126   *The Sociology of Pottery*

Cherry, J.F., and J.L. Davis
  1982   'The Cyclades and the Greek Mainland in LC I: The Evidence of the Pottery'. *American Journal of Archaeology* 86:333-41.
Childe, V.G.
  1965   'Rotary Motion'. Pp. 187-215 in *A History of Technology*, vol. 1. Ed. C. Singer, E.J. Holmyard and A.R. Hall. Reprint of 1954 edn, London: Oxford University Press.
Clamer, C., and D. Ussishkin
  1977   'A Canaanite Temple at Tell Lachish'. *Biblical Archaeologist* 40:71-76.
Clarke, D.L.
  1978   *Analytical Archaeology.* 2nd edn. London: Methuen.
Cleland, C.E.
  1972   'From Sacred to Profane: Style Drift in the Decoration of Jesuit Finger Rings'. *American Antiquity* 37:202-10.
Cohen, R.
  1974   'Har Yeruham'. *Israel Exploration Journal* 24:133-34.
Combès, J.L., and A. Louis
  1967   *Les Potiers de Djerba.* Tunis: Publication du Centre des Arts et Traditions Populaires.
Cornelius, J.
  1981   'A Bird's Eye View of Trade in Ancient Ugarit'. *Journal of Northwest Semitic Languages* 9:13-31.
Coulson, W.D.E., and N.C. Wilkie
  1986   'Ptolemaic and Roman Kilns in the Western Nile Delta'. *Bulletin of the American Schools of Oriental Research* 263:61-75.
Cross, F.M., Jr
  1954   'The Evolution of the Proto-Canaanite Alphabet'. *Bulletin of the American Schools of Oriental Research* 134:15-24.
  1969   'Judean Stamps'. *Eretz Israel* 9:20-22.
Crossland, L.B., and M. Posnausky
  1978   'Pottery, People and Trade at Begho, Ghana'. Pp. 77-89 in *The Spatial Organization of Culture*. Ed. I. Hodder. London: Duckworth.
Crowfoot, G.M.
  1932   'Pots, Ancient and Modern'. *Palestine Exploration Fund Quarterly Statement* 1932:179-87.
  1938   'Mat Impressions on Pot Bases'. *Liverpool Annals of Archaeology and Anthropology* 25:3-11.
Curtis, F.
  1962   'The Utility Pottery Industry of Bailén, Southern Spain'. *American Anthropologist* 64:486-503.
Dalton, G.
  1969   'Theoretical Issues in Economic Anthropology'. *Current Anthropology* 10:63-102.
David, N.
  1972   'On the Life Span of Pottery, Type Frequencies, and Archaeological Inference'. *American Antiquity* 37:141-42.
David, N., and H. Hennig
  1972   *The Ethnography of Pottery: A Fulani Case Study Seen in Archaeological Perspective.* McCaleb Modules, 21. Reading, MA: Addison-Wesley.

Davies, N.G.
1930   *The Tomb of Ken-amūn at Thebes*. The Metropolitan Museum of
        Art Expedition, 11. New York: The Metropolitan Museum of Art.
Davis, D.D.
1983   'Investigating the Diffusion of Stylistic Innovations'. Pp. 53-89 in
        Advances in Archaeological Method and Theory, vol. 6. ed. M.B.
        Schiffer. New York: Academic Press.
Dayton, J.E.
1972   'Midianite and Edomite Pottery'. Pp. 25-33 in *Proceedings of the
        Fifth Seminar for Arabian Studies, Sept. 22-23, 1971*. London: Semi-
        nar for Arabian Studies.
DeBoer, W.R.
1974   'Ceramic Longevity and Archaeological Interpretation: An
        Example From the Upper Ucayalo, Peru'. *American Antiquity*
        39:335-43.
DeBoer, W.R., and D.W. Lathrap
1979   'The Making and Breaking of Shipibo-Conibo Ceramics'. Pp. 102-38
        in *Ethnoarchaeology: Implications of Ethnography for Archaeol-
        ogy*. Ed. C. Kramer. New York: Columbia University Press.
Deetz, J.A.
1967   *Invitation to Archaeology*. Garden City, NY: Natural History
        Press.
Deetz, J.A., and E.S. Dethlefen
1965   'The Doppler Effect and Archaeology: A Consideration of the
        Spatial Aspects of Seriation'. *Southwestern Journal of Anthropol-
        ogy* 21:196-206. Reprinted pp. 133-44 in *Experimental Archaeology*,
        ed. D. Ingersoll, J.E. Yellen and W. Macdonald. New York:
        Columbia University Press, 1977.
1967   'Death's Head, Cherub, Urn and Willow'. *Natural History* 76:29-
        37.
Delcroix, G., and J.-L. Huot
1972   'Les fours dits "de potier" dans l'orient ancient'. *Syria* 49:35-95.
Demsky, A.
1966   'The House of Achzib'. *Israel Exploration Journal* 16:211-15.
Dethlefsen, E.S., and J.A. Deetz
1966   'Death's Heads, Cherubs, and Willow Trees: Experimental
        Archaeology in Colonial Cemeteries'. *American Antiquity* 31:502-
        10.
Dever, W.G.
1969   'Khalit el-Fûl'. *Revue Biblique* 76:572-76.
1976   'The Beginning of the Middle Bronze Age in Syria-Palestine'. Pp.
        3-38 in *Magnalia Dei: The Mighty Acts of God. Essays on the Bible
        and Archaeology in Memory of G. Ernest Wright*. Ed. F.M. Cross,
        W.E. Lemke and P.D. Miller, Jr. Garden City, NY: Doubleday.
Dever, W.G. *et al.*
1971   'Further Excavations at Gezer, 1967–1971'. *Biblical Archaeologist*
        34:94-132.
Donnan, C.B.
1971   'Ancient Peruvian Potters' Marks and their Interpretation
        through Ethnographic Analogy'. *American Antiquity* 36:460-66.

1973   *Moche Occupation of the Santa Valley, Peru.* University of California Publications in Anthropology, 8. Berkeley: University of California Press.

Dorsey, D.A.
1988   'Travel; Transportation'. Pp. 891-97 in *The International Standard Bible Encyclopaedia*, vol. 4. Ed. G.W. Bromiley. Grand Rapids, MI: Eerdmans.
Forthcoming *The Roads and Highways of Ancient Israel.* Baltimore: Johns Hopkins University Press.

Dothan, M.
1971   *Ashdod 2-3: The Second and Third Seasons of Excavations, 1963, 1965.* Atiqot 9-10 (English Series).
1975   ''Afula'. Pp. 32-36 in *Encyclopedia of Archaeological Excavations in the Holy Land*, vol. 1. Ed. M. Avi-Yonah. Englewood Cliffs, NJ: Prentice-Hall.
1979   'Ashdod at the End of the Late Bronze Age and the Beginning of the Iron Age'. Pp. 125-34 in *Symposia: Celebrating the Seventy-Fifth Anniversary of the Founding of the American Schools of Oriental Research (1900–1975).* Ed. F.M. Cross. Cambridge, MA: American Schools of Oriental Research.

Dothan, M., and D. Conrad
1978   ''Akko, 1978'. *Israel Exploration Journal* 28:264-66.
1979   ''Akko, 1979'. *Israel Exploration Journal* 29:227-28.
1983   ''Akko, 1982'. *Israel Exploration Journal* 33:113-14.
1984   ''Akko, 1983'. *Israel Exploration Journal* 34:189-190.

Dothan, M., and D.N. Freedman
1967   *Ashdod 1: The First Season of Excavations, 1962. Atiqot* 6 (English Series).

Dothan, M., and Y. Porath
1982   *Ashdod 4: Excavation of Area M. Atiqot* 15 (English Series).

Dothan, T.
1981   'Deir el-Balaḥ, 1979, 1980'. *Israel Exploration Journal* 31:126-31.
1982   *The Philistines and their Material Culture.* Revised translation from 1967 Hebrew edn. New Haven: Yale University Press.
1989   'The Arrival of the Sea Peoples: Cultural Diversity in Early Iron Age Canaan'. Pp. 1-14 in *Recent Excavations in Israel: Studies in Iron Age Archaeology.* Ed. S. Gitin and W.G. Dever. The Annual of the American Schools of Oriental Research, 49. Winona Lake, IN: Eisenbrauns.

Duncan, J.G.
1930   *Corpus of Dated Palestinian Pottery.* British School of Archaeology in Egypt Publication, 49. London: British School of Archaeology in Egypt.

Edelstein, G., and J. Glass
1973   'The Origin of Philistine Pottery Based on Petrographic Analysis'. Pp. 125-32 in *Excavations and Studies: Essays in Honour of Professor S. Yeivin.* Ed. Y. Aharoni. Tel Aviv: Carta (Hebrew, English summary p. xvi).

Edwards, I., and L. Jacobs
1986   'Experiments with Stone "Pottery Wheel" Bearings—Notes on the Use of Rotation in the Production of Ancient Pottery'. *Newsletter, Department of Pottery Technology, University of Leiden* 4:49-55.

Edwards, W.I., and E.R. Segnit
1984   'Pottery Technology at the Chalcolithic Site of Teleilat Ghassul (Jordan)'. *Archaeometry* 26:69-77.

Ehrich, R.W.
1965   'Ceramics and Man: A Cultural Perspective'. Pp. 1-19 in *Ceramics and Man*. Ed. F.R. Matson. Viking Fund Publications in Anthropology, 41. New York: Wenner-Gren Foundation for Anthropological Research.

Einsler, L.
1914   'Das Töpferhandwerk bei Bauernfrauen von Ramallah und Umgegend'. *Zeitschrift des Deutschen Palästina-Vereins* 37:249-60.

Ellison, R.
1984   'The Uses of Pottery'. *Iraq* 46:63-68.

Engelbrecht, W.
1974   'The Iroquois: Archaeological Patterning on the Tribal Level'. *World Archaeology* 6:52-65.

Esse, D.L.
1982   'A Chronological Mirage: Reflections on Early Bronze IC in Palestine'. *Journal of Near Eastern Studies* 43:317-30.

Falconer, S.E.
1987   'Village Pottery Production and Exchange: A Jordan Valley Perspective'. Pp. 251-59 in *Studies in the History and Archaeology of Jordan*, vol. 3. Ed. A. Hadidi. New York: Routledge & Kegan Paul.

Falconer, S.E., M.C. Metzger, and B. Magness-Gardiner
1984   'Preliminary Report of the First Season of the Tell el-Hayyat Project'. *Bulletin of the American Schools of Oriental Research* 255:49-74.

Fisher, C.S.
1929   *The Excavations of Armageddon*. Oriental Institute Communications, 4. Chicago: University of Chicago Press.

Forshey, H.O.
1983   'Incised Jar Handles from Tell Halif'. *Lahav Newsletter* 23:1-3. Privately circulated by the Lahav Research Project, Mississippi State University, MS.

1984   'Potter's (*sic*) Marks and the Development of the Alphabet'. Unpublished paper presented at the annual meeting of the American Schools of Oriental Research, Chicago.

Foster, G.M.
1956   'Pottery-Making in Bengal'. *Southwestern Journal of Anthropology* 12:395-405.

1959   'The Potter's Wheel: An Analysis of Idea and Artifact in Invention'. *Southwestern Journal of Anthropology* 15:99-117.

1960   'Life Expectancy of Utilitarian Pottery in Tzintzuntzan, Michoacán, Mexico'. *American Antiquity* 25:606-609.

1965   'The Sociology of Pottery: Questions and Hypotheses Arising from Contemporary Mexican Work'. Pp. 43-61 in *Ceramics and Man*. Ed. F.R. Matson. Viking Fund Publications in Anthropology, 41. New York: Wenner-Gren Foundation for Anthropological Research.

130   *The Sociology of Pottery*

Frankel, D.
1975   'The Pot Marks of Vounous: Clustering Techniques, their Problems and Potential'. *Opuscula Atheniensia* 11:37-51.
Franken, H.J.
1969   *Excavations at Tell Deir 'Allā 1: A Stratigraphical and Analytical Study of the Early Iron Age Pottery*. Leiden: Brill.
1971   'Analysis of Methods of Potmaking in Archaeology'. *Harvard Theological Review* 64:227-55.
1982   'A Technological Study of Iron Age I Pottery from Tell Deir 'Allā'. Pp. 141-44 in *Studies in the History and Archaeology of Jordan*. Ed. A. Hadidi. Amman: Department of Antiquities.
Fry, R.E.
1979   'The Economics of Pottery at Tikal, Guatemala: Models of Exchange for Serving Vessels'. *American Antiquity* 44:494-512.
1980   'Models of Exchange for Major Shape Classes of Lowland Maya Pottery'. Pp. 3-18 in *Models and Methods in Regional Exchange*. Ed. R.E. Fry. Society for American Archaeology Papers, 1. Washington, DC: Society for American Archaeology.
Fry, R.E., and S.C. Cox
1974   'The Structure of Ceramic Exchange at Tikal, Guatemala'. *World Archaeology* 6:209-25.
Furumark, A.
1972   *Mycenaean Pottery 2: Chronology*. Stockholm: Skrifter utgivna av Svenska Institutet i Athen.
Garstang, J.
1934   'Jericho: City and Necropolis, Fourth Report'. *Annals of Archaeology and Anthropology* 21:99-136.
Gerstenblith, P.
1983   *The Levant at the Beginning of the Middle Bronze Age*. American Schools of Oriental Research Dissertation Series, 5. Winona Lake, IN: Eisenbrauns.
Geva, S.
1982   *Tell Jerishe: The Sukenik Excavations of the Middle Bronze Age Fortifications*. Qedem 15. Jerusalem: Institute of Archaeology, Hebrew University.
Gittlen, B.M.
1975   'Cypriote White Slip Pottery in its Palestinian Stratigraphic Context'. Pp. 111-20 in *The Archaeology of Cyprus: Recent Developments*. Ed. N. Robertson. Park Ridge, IL: Noyes.
1977   'Studies in the Late Cypriote Pottery Found in Palestine'. Ph.D. dissertation, University of Pennsylvania. Ann Arbor, MI: University Microfilms.
1981   'The Cultural and Chronological Implications of the Cypro-Palestinian Trade during the Late Bronze Age'. *Bulletin of the American Schools of Oriental Research* 241:49-59.
Glanzman, W.
1983   'Xeroradiographic Examination of Pottery Manufacturing Techniques: A Test Case from the Baq'ah Valley, Jordan'. *MASCA Journal* 2:163-69.
Glanzman, W.D. and S.J. Fleming
1986   'Technology: Fabricating Methods'. Pp. 164-77 in *The Late Bronze and Early Iron Ages of Central Transjordan: The Baq'ah Valley*

Project, 1977–1981, by P.E. McGovern. University Museum Monograph. Philadelphia: The University Museum, University of Pennsylvania.

Glock, A.E.
1982   'Ceramic Ethno-Techniculture'. Pp. 145-51 in *Studies in the History and Archaeology of Jordan*. Ed. A. Hadidi. Amman: Department of Antiquities.
1983   'The Use of Ethnography in an Archaeological Research Design'. Pp. 171-79 in *The Quest for the Kingdom of God: Studies in Honor of George E. Mendenhall*. Ed. H.B. Huffmon, F.A. Spina and A.R.W. Green. Winona Lake, IN: Eisenbrauns.

Gordon, C.
1956   'Ugaritic Guilds and Homeric ΔΗΜΙΟΕΡΓΟΙ'. Pp. 136-43 in *The Aegean and the Near East: Studies Presented to Hetty Goldman*. Ed. S.S. Weinberg. Locust Valley, NY: J.J. Augustin.

Gould, R.A.
1978   'Beyond Analogy in Ethnoarchaeology'. Pp. 249-93 in *Explorations in Ethnoarchaeology*. Ed. R.A. Gould. School of American Research Advanced Seminar Series. Albuquerque: University of New Mexico Press.
1980   *Living Archaeology*. Cambridge: Cambridge University Press.

Grant, E.
1934   *Rumeileh: Being Ain Shems Excavations (Palestine), Part 3*. Biblical and Kindred Studies, 5. Haverford, PA: Haverford College.

Grant, E., and G.E. Wright
1939   *Ain Shems Excavations (Palestine), Part 5 (Text)*. Biblical and Kindred Studies, 8. Haverford, PA: Haverford College.

Groves, M.
1960   'Moto Pottery'. *The Journal of the Polynesian Society* 69:3-22.

Guest-Papamanoli, A.
1983   'Keramiki: Mia Panarchaia Techni'. *Archeologia* 9:53-58.

Gunneweg, J., I. Perlman, and Z. Meshel
1985   'The Origin of the Pottery of Kuntillet 'Ajrud'. *Israel Exploration Journal* 35:270-83.

Gunneweg, J., T. Dothan, I. Perlman, and S. Gitin
1986   'On the Origin of Pottery from Tel Miqne-Ekron'. *Bulletin of the American Schools of Oriental Research* 264:3-27.

Gunneweg, J., I. Perlman and F. Asaro
1987   'A Canaanite Jar from Enkomi'. *Israel Exploration Journal* 37:168-72.

Guy, P.L.O.
1938   *Megiddo Tombs*. University of Chicago Oriental Institute Publication, 33. Chicago: University of Chicago Press.

Haaland, R.
1978   'Ethnographical Observations of Pottery-Making in Darfur, Western Sudan, with some Reflections on Archaeological Interpretations'. Pp. 47-61 in *New Directions in Scandinavian Archaeology*. Ed. K. Kristiansen and C. Pauludan-Müller. Studies in Scandinavian Prehistory and Early History, 1. Copenhagen: National Museum of Denmark.

Halligan, J.M.
1983   'The Role of the Peasant in the Amarna Period'. Pp. 15-24 in
        Palestine in Transition. Ed. D.N. Freedman and D.F. Graf. The
        Social World of Biblical Antiquity Series, 2. Sheffield: Almond.
Halpern, B.
1983   *The Emergence of Israel in Canaan*. Society of Biblical Literature
        Monograph Series, 29. Chico, CA: Scholars.
Hammond, P.H.
1971   'Ceramic Technology of South-West Asia, Syria-Palestine: Iron
        IIb, Hebron'. *Science and Archaeology* 5:11-21.
Hampe, R., and A. Winter
1962   *Bei Töpfern und Töpferinnen in Kreta, Messenien, und Zypern*.
        Mainz: Verlag des Römisch-Germanischen Zentralmuseums.
1965   *Bei Töpfern und Zieglern in Süditalien, Sizilien, und Griechen-
        land*. Mainz: Verlag des Römisch-Germanischen Zentral-
        museums.
Hankey, V.
1967   'Mycenaean Pottery in the Middle East: Notes since 1951'. *Annual
        of the British School at Athens* 62:107-47.
1968   'Pottery Making at Beit Shebab, Lebanon'. *Palestine Exploration
        Quarterly* 100:27-32.
1970   'Mycenaean Trade with the Southeastern Mediterranean'.
        Mélanges de l'Université Saint-Joseph 46:24-26.
1981   'Imported Vessels of the Late Bronze Age at High Places'. Pp. 108-
        17 in *Temples and High Places in Biblical Times*. Ed. A. Biran.
        Jerusalem: The Nelson Glueck School of Biblical Archaeology of
        Hebrew Union College–Jewish Institute of Religion.
Har-El, M.
1981   'Jerusalem and Judea: Roads and Fortifications'. *Biblical Archae-
        ologist* 44:8-19.
Heltzer, M.
1965   'The Organization of Craftsmanship in Ugarit'. *Palestinský
        Sbornik* 13:47-60 (in Russian, English summary pp. 59-60).
1969   'Problems of the Social History of Syria in the Late Bronze Age'.
        Pp. 31-46 in *La Siria nel Tardo Bronze*. Ed. M. Liverani. Rome:
        Centro per le antichità e la storia dell'arte del vicino oriente.
1982   *The Internal Organization of the Kingdom of Ugarit*. Wiesbaden:
        Ludwig Reichert.
Hennessy, J.B., and A. Millett
1963   'Spectrographic Analysis of the Foreign Pottery from Royal Tombs
        of Abydos and Early Bronze Age Pottery of Palestine'. *Archaeome-
        try* 6:10-17.
Henrickson, E.F., and M.M.A. McDonald
1983   'Ceramic Form and Function: An Ethnographic Search and an
        Archaeological Application'. *American Anthropologist* 85:630-43.
Herr, L.G.
1988   'Tripartite Pillared Buildings and the Market Place in Iron Age
        Palestine'. *Bulletin of the American Schools of Oriental Research*
        272:47-67.

Hestrin, R.
1975 'Beth Yerah (Kh. el-Kerak)'. Pp. 253-62 in *Encyclopedia of Archaeological Excavations in the Holy Land,* vol. 1. Ed. M. Avi-Yonah. Englewood Cliffs, NJ: Prentice-Hall.

Hill, J.N.
1977 'Individual Variability in Ceramics and the Study of Prehistoric Social Organization'. Pp. 55-108 in *The Individual in Prehistory: Studies of Variability in Style in Prehistoric Technologies.* Ed. J.N. Hill and J. Gunn. New York: Academic Press.
1985 'Style: A Conceptual Evolutionary Framework'. Pp. 362-85 in *Decoding Prehistoric Ceramics.* Ed. B.A. Nelson. Carbondale: Southern Illinois University Press.

Hodder, I.
1978 'Social Organization: The Development of some Tentative Hypotheses in Terms of Material Culture'. Pp. 199-269 in *The Spatial Organization of Culture.* Ed. I. Hodder. London: Duckworth.

Hodder, I., and C. Orton
1976 *Spatial Analysis in Archaeology.* Cambridge: Cambridge University Press.

Hodges, H.
1964 *Artifacts, an Introduction to Early Materials and Technology.* London: John Baker.

Hodges, H.W.M.
1965 'Aspects of Pottery in Temperate Europe Before the Roman Empire'. Pp. 114-23 in *Ceramics and Man.* Ed. F.R. Matson. Viking Fund Publications in Anthropology, 41. New York: Wenner-Gren Foundation for Anthropological Research.

Holladay, J.S., Jr
1976 'Of Sherds and Strata: Contributions toward an Understanding of the Archaeology of the Divided Monarchy'. Pp. 253-93 in *Magnalia Dei: The Mighty Acts of God.* Ed. F.M. Cross, W.E. Lemke and P.D. Miller, Jr. Garden City, NY: Doubleday.

Holthoer, R.
1977 *New Kingdom Pharaonic Sites: The Pottery.* The Scandinavian Joint Expedition to Sudanese Nubia, 5.1. Stockholm: The Scandinavian Joint Expedition to Sudanese Nubia.

Honeyman, A.M.
1939 'The Pottery Vessels of the Old Testament'. *Palestine Exploration Quarterly* 71:76-90.

Hope, C.A.
1981 'Two Ancient Egyptian Potter's (*sic*) Wheels'. *Journal of the Society for the Study of Egyptian Antiquities* 11:127-33.
1982 *Ancient Egyptian Pottery.* Melbourne: Royal Melbourne Institute of Technology.

Hopkins, I.W.J.
1980 'The City Region in Roman Palestine'. *Palestine Exploration Quarterly* 112:19-32.

Impey, O.R., and M. Pollard
1985 'A Multivariate Metrical Study of Ceramics Made by Three Potters'. *Oxford Journal of Archaeology* 4:157-64.

134   *The Sociology of Pottery*

Isserlin, B.S.J., and O. Tufnell
1950   'The City Deposits at Tell ed-Duweir: A Summary of the Stratification'. *Palestine Exploration Quarterly* 82:81-91.
James, F.W.
1962   'The Pottery of the Old Testament'. *Expedition* 5:36-41.
1966   *The Iron Age at Beth Shan: A Study of Levels VI–IV*. Philadelphia: University Museum, University of Pennsylvania.
Johnston, R.H.
1974a 'The Biblical Potter'. *Biblical Archaeologist* 37:86-106.
1974b 'The Cypriote Potter'. Pp. 131-39 in *American Expedition to Idalion, Cyprus—First Preliminary Report: Seasons of 1971 and 1972*. Ed. L.E. Stager, A. Walker and G.E. Wright. Supplement to the *Bulletin of the American Schools of Oriental Research*, 18. Cambridge, MA: American Schools of Oriental Research.
1977   'The Development of the Potter's Wheel: An Analytical and Synthesizing Study'. Pp. 169-210 in *Material Culture: Styles, Organization, and Dynamics of Technology*. Ed. H. Lechtman and R.S. Merrill. St Paul: West.
1984   'An Abandoned Pottery at Guellala on the Island of Djerba, Tunisia: A Hermeneutic Approach to Ethnoarchaeology'. Pp. 81-94 in *Pots and Potters: Current Approaches in Ceramic Archaeology*. Ed. P.M. Rice. University of California Institute of Archaeology Monograph, 24. Los Angeles: University of California.
1986   'Potter; Pottery'. Pp. 913-21 in *The International Standard Bible Encyclopaedia*, vol. 3. Ed. G.W. Bromiley. Grand Rapids, MI: Eerdmans.
Kalsbeek, J., and G. London
1978   'A Late Second Millennium BC Potting Puzzle'. *Bulletin of the American Schools of Oriental Research* 232:47-56.
Kaplan, J.
1965   'Skin Bottles and Pottery Imitations'. *Palestine Exploration Quarterly* 97:144-52.
1972   'The Archaeology and History of Tel Aviv–Jaffa'. *Biblical Archaeologist* 35:66-95.
Kelso, J.L.
1948   *The Ceramic Vocabulary of the Old Testament*. Supplement to the *Bulletin of the American Schools of Oriental Research*, 5-6. Cambridge, MA: American Schools of Oriental Research.
Kelso, J.L., and J.P. Thorley
1943   'The Potter's Technique at Tell Beit Mirsim, Particularly in Stratum A'. Pp. 86-142 in *The Excavation of Tell Beit Mirsim*, vol. 3. *The Iron Age*, by W.F. Albright. Annual of the American Schools of Oriental Research, 21-22 for 1941–1943. Cambridge, MA: American Schools of Oriental Research.
Kenyon, K.M.
1979   *Archaeology in the Holy Land*. 4th edn. New York: W.W. Norton.
1981   *Excavations at Jericho*, vol. 3. *The Architecture and Stratigraphy of the Tell*. London: British School of Archaeology in Jerusalem.
Kenyon, K.M., and T.A. Holland
1983   *Excavations at Jericho*, vol. 5. *The Pottery Phases of the Tell and Other Finds*. London: British School of Archaeology in Jerusalem.

Killebrew, A.
1982   'The Pottery Workshop in Ancient Egyptian Reliefs and Paintings'.
        Pp. 60-100 in *Papers for Discussion I, 1981–1982.* Ed. S. Groll, and
        H.E. Stein. Jerusalem: Department of Egyptology, Hebrew Uni-
        versity.
Kochavi, M.
1963   'Har Yeruḥam'. *Israel Exploration Journal* 13:141-42.
1978   'Yeruḥam, Mount'. Pp. 1219-20 in *Encyclopedia of Archaeological
        Excavations in the Holy Land,* vol. 4. Ed. M. Avi-Yonah, and E.
        Stern. Englewood Cliffs, NJ: Prentice-Hall.
Köpke, W.
1985   *Töpferöfen: Die Brennanlagen der traditionellen Töpfereien
        Spaniens—Arten, Verbreitung und Entwicklung.* Bonn: Rudolf
        Habelt.
Kramer, C.
1982   *Village Ethnoarchaeology: Rural Iran in Archaeological Perspec-
        tive.* New York: Academic Press.
1985   'Ceramic Ethnoarchaeology'. *Annual Review of Anthropology*
        14:77-102.
Lamon, R.S., and G.M. Shipton
1939   *Megiddo: The Seasons of 1925–34, Strata I–V.* Oriental Institute
        Publication, 42. Chicago: University of Chicago Press.
Lance, H.D.
1981   *The Old Testament and the Archaeologist.* Philadelphia: Fortress.
Lapp, P.W.
1970   'The Tell Deir 'Allā Challenge to Palestinian Archaeology'. *Vetus
        Testamentum* 20:243-56.
1975   *The Tale of the Tell.* Pittsburgh Theological Monograph Series, 5.
        Pittsburgh: Pickwick.
Larson, B.K.
1982   'The Structure and Function of Village Markets in Contemporary
        Egypt'. *Journal of the American Research Center in Egypt* 19:131-
        44.
Leeuw, S.E. van der
1977   'Towards a Study of the Economics of Pottery Making'. Pp. 68-76 in
        Ex Horreo. Ed. B.L. Van Beek, R.W. Brandt and W. Groenman-
        van Waateringe. Amsterdam: Universiteit van Amsterdam.
Leonard, A., Jr
1976   'The Nature and Extent of the Aegean Presence in West Asia
        During the Late Bronze Age'. Ph.D. dissertation, University of
        Chicago.
1981   'Considerations of Morphological Variation in the Mycenaean
        Pottery from the Southeastern Mediterranean'. *Bulletin of the
        American Schools of Oriental Research* 241:87-101.
1987   'The Significance of the Mycenaean Pottery Found East of the Jor-
        dan River'. Pp. 261-66 in *Studies in the History and Archaeology of
        Jordan,* vol. 3. Ed. A. Hadidi. New York: Routledge & Kegan Paul.
Liebowitz, H.
1981   'Excavations at Tel Yin'am: The 1976 and 1977 Seasons: Prelimi-
        nary Report'. *Bulletin of the American Schools of Oriental
        Research* 243:79-94.

Liebowitz, H., and R. Folk
1984   'The Dawn of Iron Smelting in Palestine: The Late Bronze Age Smelter at Tel Yin'am (*sic*): Preliminary Report'. *Journal of Field Archaeology* 11:265-80.
Linares de Sapir, O.
1969   'Diola Pottery of the Fogny and the Kasa'. *Expedition* 11/3:2-11.
Lisse, P., and A. Louis
1956   *Les potiers de Nabeul: Etude de sociologie tunisienne*. Publications de l'Institut de Belles Lettres Arabes, 23. Tunis: Institut de Belles Lettres Arabes.
Litto, G.
1976   *South American Folk Pottery*. New York: Watson-Guptill.
Llorens Artigas, J., and J. Corredor-Matheos
1974   *Spanish Folk Ceramics*. New York: Watson-Guptill.
Loebert, H.W.
1984   'Types of Potter's Wheels and the Spread of the Spindle Wheel in Germany'. Pp. 203-22 in *The Many Dimensions of Pottery: Ceramics in Archaeology and Anthropology*. Ed. S.E. van der Leeuw and A.C. Pritchard. Universiteit van Amsterdam Albert Egges van Griffen Instituut voor Prae- en Protohistorie Cingvla, 7. Amsterdam: Universiteit van Amsterdam.
London, G.A.
1987a   'Cypriote Potters: Past and Present'. Pp. 319-22 in *Report of the Department of Antiquities, Cyprus*. Nicosia: Department of Antiquities.
1987b   'Regionalism in Traditional Cypriot Ceramics'. *Newsletter, Department of Pottery Technology, University of Leiden*, 5:125-36.
1989a   'A Comparison of Two Contemporaneous Lifestyles of the Late Second Millennium BCE'. *Bulletin of the American Schools of Oriental Research* 273:37-55.
1989b   'Past and Present: The Village Potters of Cyprus'. *Biblical Archaeologist* 52:219-29.
London, G.A., F. Egoumenidou and V. Karageorghis
1989   *Traditional Pottery in Cyprus*. Mainz: von Zabern.
Longacre, W.A.
1981   'Kalinga Pottery: An Ethnoarchaeological Study'. Pp. 49-66 in *Patterns of the Past*. Ed. I. Hodder, G. Isaac, and N. Hammond. Cambridge: Cambridge University Press.
1985   'Pottery Use-Life among the Kalinga, Northern Luzon, the Philippines'. Pp. 334-46 in *Decoding Prehistoric Ceramics*. Ed. B.A. Nelson. Carbondale, IL: Southern Illinois University Press.
Longacre, W.A., K.L. Knamme and M. Kobayashi
1988   'Southwestern Pottery Standardization: An Ethnoarchaeological View from the Philippines'. *The Kiva* 53: 101-12.
Loud, G.
1948   *Megiddo 2: Seasons of 1935–39*. Oriental Institute Publication, 62. Chicago: University of Chicago Press.
Macalister, R.A.S.
1912   *The Excavation of Gezer*, 3 vols. London: Palestine Exploration Fund.

McClellan, T.L.
1975   'Quantitative Studies in the Iron Age Pottery of Palestine'. Ph.D. dissertation, University of Pennsylvania. Ann Arbor, MI: University Microfilms International.

McCown, C.C.
1947   *Tell en-Naṣbeh 1*. Berkeley: Palestine Institute of the Pacific School of Religion.

McGovern, P.E.
1986   'Stylistic Change: Contrasting Studies from Southwest and Southeast Asia'. Pp. 35-52 in *Technology and Style*. Ed. W.D. Kingery. *Ceramics and Civilisation*, vol. 2. Columbus, OH: American Ceramic Society.

Maisler, B., M. Stekelis and M. Avi-Yonah
1952   'The Excavations at Beth Yarah (Khirbet el-Kerak) 1944–1946'. *Israel Exploration Journal* 2:165-73.

Mallowan, M.E.L.
1939   'Phoenician Carrying Trade, Syria'. *Antiquity* 13:86-87.

Matson, F.R.
1965   'Ceramic Ecology: An Approach to the Study of the Early Cultures of the Near East'. Pp. 202-17 in *Ceramics and Man*. Ed. F.R. Matson. Viking Fund Publications in Anthropology, 41. New York: Wenner-Gren Foundation for Anthropological Research.
1966   'Power and Fuel Resources in the Ancient Near East'. *Advancement of Science* 23:146-53.
1972   'Ceramic Studies'. Pp. 200-204 in *The Minnesota Messenian Expedition: Reconstruction of a Bronze Age Regional Environment*. Ed. W.A. McDonald and G.R. Rapp, Jr. Minneapolis: The University of Minnesota Press.
1973   'The Potters of Chalkis'. Pp. 117-42 in *Classics and the Classical Tradition*. Ed. E.N. Borza and R.W. Carruba. University Park: Pennsylvania State University Press.
1974   'The Archaeological Present: Near Eastern Village Potters at Work'. *American Journal of Archaeology* 78:345-47.

Mazar, A.
1988   'A Note on Canaanite Jars from Enkomi'. *Israel Exploration Journal* 38:224-26.

Mendelsohn, I.
1940   'Guilds in Ancient Palestine'. *Bulletin of the American Schools of Oriental Research* 80:17-21.

Mershen, B.
1985   'Recent Hand-Made Pottery from Northern Jordan'. *Berytus* 33:75-87.

Meyers, C.
1983   'Of Seasons and Soldiers: A Typological Appraisal of the Premonarchic Tribes of Galilee'. *Bulletin of the American Schools of Oriental Research* 252:47-59.

Mommsen, H., J. Perlman and J. Yellin
1984   'The Provenience of the *lmlk* jars'. *Israel Exploration Journal* 34:89-113.

Muhly, J.D.
1982   'How Iron Technology Changed the Ancient World'. *Biblical Archaeology Review* 8:40-54.

Na'aman, N.
  1986   'Hezekiah's Fortified Cities and the *LMLK* Stamps'. *Bulletin of the American Schools of Oriental Research* 261:5-21.
Nicholson, P.T., and H.L. Patterson
  1985a   'Ethnoarchaeology in Egypt: The Ballas Pottery Project'. *Archaeology* 38/3:53-59.
  1985b   'Pottery Making in Upper Egypt: An Ethnoarchaeological Study'. *World Archaeology* 17:222-39.
Nicklin, K.
  1971   'Stability and Innovation in Pottery Manufacture'. *World Archaeology* 3:13-48.
  1979   'The Location of Pottery Manufacture'. *Man* 14:436-58.
Nicolaou, K.
  1982   'The Mycenaeans in the East'. Pp. 121-26 in *Studies in the History and Archaeology of Jordan*. Ed. A. Hadidi. Amman: Department of Antiquities.
Noble, J.V.
  1965   *The Techniques of Painted Attic Pottery*. New York: Watson-Guptill.
Ochsenschlager, E.L.
  1974   'Modern Potters at Al-Hiba With Some Reflections on the Excavated Early Dynastic Pottery'. Pp. 149-57 in *Ethnoarchaeology*. Ed. C.B. Donnan and C.W. Clewlow, Jr. Monograph, 4, Archaeological Survey. Los Angeles: Institute of Archaeology, University of California.
Okpoko, A.I.
  1987   'Pottery Making in Igbo Land, Eastern Nigeria: An Ethnoarchaeological Study'. *Proceedings of the Prehistoric Society* 53:445-55.
Oren, E.
  1987   'The "Ways of Horus" in North Sinai'. Pp. 69-119 in *Egypt, Israel, Sinai: Archaeological and Historical Relationships*. Ed. A.F. Rainey. Tel Aviv: Tel Aviv University.
Parr, P.J.
  1982   'Contacts between North West Arabia and Jordan in the Late Bronze and Iron Ages'. Pp. 127-33 in *Studies in the History and Archaeology of Jordan*. Ed. A. Hadidi. Amman: Department of Antiquities.
Parr, P.J., G.L. Harding and J.F. Dayton
  1970   'Preliminary Survey in NW Arabia, 1968'. *Bulletin of the Institute of Archaeology 8 and 9: 1968–69*: 193-242.
Peacock, D.P.S.
  1981   'Archaeology, Ethnology and Ceramic Production'. Pp. 187-94 in *Production and Distribution: A Ceramic Viewpoint*. Ed. H. Howard and E.L. Morris. BAR International Series, 120. Oxford: British Archaeological Reports.
  1982   *Pottery in the Roman World: An Ethnoarchaeological Approach*. London: Longman.
Perlman, I., and F. Asaro
  1982   'Provenience Studies on Pottery of Stratum 11 and 10'. Pp. 70-90 in *Ashdod 4: Excavation of Area M*, by M. Dothan and Y. Porath. *Atiqot* 15 (English Series).

Petrie, W.M.F.
1891   *Tell el Hesy (Lachish).* London: Palestine Exploration Fund.
1931   *Ancient Gaza 1.* British School of Archaeology in Egypt Publication, 53. London: British School of Archaeology in Egypt.
1952   'City of Shepherd Kings'. Pp. 3-21 in *City of Shepherd Kings and Ancient Gaza 5,* by W.M.F. Petrie, E.J.H. Mackay and M.A. Murray. British School of Egyptian Archaeology Publication, 64. London: British School of Egyptian Archaeology.

Plog, S.
1976   'Measurement of Prehistoric Interaction between Communities'. Pp. 255-72 in *The Early Mesoamerican Village.* Ed. K.V. Flannery. New York: Academic Press.
1980   *Stylistic Variation in Prehistoric Ceramics.* Cambridge: Cambridge University Press.

Polyani, K.
1975   'Traders and Trade'. Pp. 133-54 in *Ancient Civilizations and Trade.* Ed. G.A. Sabloff and C.C. Lamberg-Karlovsky. Albuquerque: University of New Mexico Press.

Potts, D.
1981   'The Potter's (*sic*) Marks of Tepe Yahya'. *Paléorient* 7/1:107-22.

Pritchard, J.B.
1975   *Sarepta: A Preliminary Report on the Iron Age.* Philadelphia: University Museum.
1978   *Recovering Sarepta, a Phoenician City.* Princeton: Princeton University Press.

Rainey, A.F.
1962   'The Social Stratification at Ugarit'. Ph.D. dissertation, Brandeis University. Ann Arbor MI: University Microfilms.
1982   'Wine from the Royal Vineyards'. *Bulletin of the American Schools of Oriental Research* 245:57-62 (= *Eretz Israel* 16 [1982]:177-81 [Hebrew, English summary p. 258*]).
1983   'The Biblical Shephelah of Judah'. *Bulletin of the American Schools of Oriental Research* 251:1-22.

Randall-Maciver, D.
1905   'The Manufacture of Pottery in Upper Egypt'. *Journal of the Anthropological Institute of Great Britain and Ireland* 35:20-29.

Rands, R.L.
1967   'Ceramic Technology and Trade in the Palenque Region, Mexico'. Pp. 137-51 in *American Historical Anthropology.* Ed. C. Riley and W.W. Taylor. Carbondale: Southern Illinois University Press.

Rathje, W.L.
1975   'The Last Tango in Mayapan: A Tentative Trajectory of Production–Distribution Systems'. Pp. 409-48 in *Ancient Civilization and Trade.* Ed. J.A. Sabloff and C.C. Lamberg-Karlovsky. Albuquerque: University of New Mexico Press.

Reina, R.E., and R.M. Hill
1978   *The Traditional Pottery of Guatemala.* The Texas Pan American Series. Austin: University of Texas Press.

Renfrew, A.C.
1975   'Trade as Action at a Distance: Questions of Integration and Communication'. Pp. 3-59 in *Ancient Civilization and Trade.* Ed.

J.A. Sabloff and C.C. Lamberg-Karlovsky. Albuquerque: University of New Mexico Press.

Rhodes, D.
1968   *Kilns: Design, Construction and Operation.* Philadelphia: Chilton.

Rice, P.M.
1981   'Evolution of Specialized Pottery: A Trial Model'. *Current Anthropology* 22:219-40.
1984   'The Archaeological Study of Specialized Pottery Production: Some Aspects of Method and Theory'. Pp. 45-54 in *Pots and Potters: Current Approaches in Ceramic Archaeology.* Ed. P.M. Rice. University of California Institute of Archaeology Monograph, 24. Los Angeles: University of California.
1987   *Pottery Analysis: A Sourcebook.* Chicago: The University of Chicago Press.

Rothenberg, B.
1972   *Timna, Valley of the Biblical Copper Mines.* London: Thames and Hudson.

Rothenberg, B., and J. Glass
1981   'Midianite Pottery'. *Eretz Israel* 15:85-114 (Hebrew, English summary pp. 80*-81*).
1983   'The Midianite Pottery'. Pp. 65-124 in *Midian, Moab and Edom: The History and Archaeology of Late Bronze and Iron Age Jordan and North-West Arabia.* Ed. J.F.A. Sawyer and D.J.A. Clines. Journal for the Study of the Old Testament Supplement Series, 24. Sheffield: JSOT.

Rye, O.S.
1981   *Pottery Technology: Principles and Reconstruction.* Manuals on Archaeology, 4. Washington: Taraxacum.

Saller, S.J.
1964   *The Excavations at Dominus Flevit (Mount Olivet, Jerusalem), Part 2: The Jebusite Burial Place.* Publications of the Studium Biblicum Franciscanum, 13. Jerusalem: Franciscan.

Saraswati, B.
1979   *Pottery-Making Cultures and Indian Civilization.* New Delhi: Abhinav.

Schiffer, M.B.
1978   'Methodological Issues in Ethnoarchaeology'. Pp. 229-47 in *Explorations in Ethno-archaeology.* Ed. R.A. Gould. School of American Research Advanced Seminar Series. Albuquerque: University of New Mexico Press.

Schumacher, G.
1908   *Tell el-Mutesellim 1, Text.* Leipzig: Rudolf Haupt.

Scott, L.
1965   'Pottery'. Pp. 376-412 in *A History of Technology,* vol. 1. Ed. C. Singer, E.J. Holmyard and A.R. Hall. Reprint of 1954 edn. London: Oxford University Press.

Seger, J.D.
1983   'The Gezer Jar Signs: New Evidence of the Earliest Alphabet'. Pp. 477-95 in *The Word of the Lord Shall Go Forth: Essays in Honor of David Noel Freedman in Celebration of His Sixtieth Birthday.* Ed. C.L. Meyers and M. O'Connor. Winona Lake, IN: Eisenbrauns.

Sellin, E.
1904   *Tell Ta'annek*. Denkschriften der Kaiserlichen Akademie der Wissenschaften in Wien, Philosophisch-historische Klasse, 50, 4. Wien: Carl Gerold's Sohn.

Sharon, I., J. Yellin, and I. Perlman
1987   'Marked Cooking Pots from Tell Qiri'. Pp. 224-35 in *Tell Qiri, a Village in the Jezreel Valley: Reports of the Archaeological Excavations 1975–1977*, by A. Ben-Tor and Y. Portugali, *et al. Qedem* 24. Jerusalem: Institute of Archaeology, Hebrew University.

Sheffer, A.
1976   'Comparative Analysis of a "Negev Ware" Textile Impression from Tell Masos'. *Tel Aviv* 3:81-88.

Shepard, A.O.
1956   *Ceramics for the Archaeologist*. Washington, DC: Carnegie Institution.

Silver, M.
1985   *Economic Structures of the Ancient Near East*. London: Croom Helm.

Slatkine, A.
1974   'Comparative Petrographic Study of Ancient Pottery Sherds from Israel'. *Museum Ha'aretz Yearbook* 15-16 (1972/73):101-11.

Smith, M.F., Jr
1985   'Toward an Economic Interpretation of Ceramics: Relating Vessel Size and Shape to Use'. Pp. 254-309 in *Decoding Prehistoric Ceramics*. Ed. B.A. Nelson. Carbondale: Southern Illinois University Press.

Smith, R.H.
1964   'The Household Lamps of Palestine in Old Testament Times'. *Biblical Archaeologist* 27:1-31.

Stanislawski, M.B.
1978   'If Pots were Mortal'. Pp. 201-27 in *Explorations in Ethnoarchaeology*. Ed. R.A. Gould. Albuquerque: University of New Mexico Press.

Stanislawski, M.B., and B.B. Stanislawski
1978   'Hopi and Hopi-Tewa Ceramic Tradition Networks'. Pp. 62-76 in *The Spatial Organization of Culture*. Ed. I. Hodder. London: Duckworth.

Starkey, J.L. and L. Harding
1932   'Beth-Pelet Cemetery'. Pp. 22-32 in *Beth-Pelet 2*, by E. MacDonald, J.L. Starkey and L. Harding. British School of Archaeology in Egypt Publication, 52. London: British School of Archaeology in Egypt.

Stillwell, A.N.
1948   *Corinth: Results of Excavations Conducted by the American Schools of Classical Studies at Athens*, vol. 15, Pt. 1. *The Potters' Quarter*. Princeton, NJ: The American Schools of Classical Studies at Athens.

Stubbings, F.H.
1951   *Mycenaean Pottery from the Levant*. Cambridge: Cambridge University Press.

Sukenik, E.L.
1940   'Note on a Pottery Vessel of the Old Testament'. *Palestine Exploration Quarterly* 1940:59-60.
Taylor, J. de P., and O. Tufnell
1930   'A Pottery Industry in Cyprus'. *Ancient Egypt* 1930:119-22.
Thompson, H.A.
1984   'The Athenian Vase-Painters and Their Neighbors'. Pp. 7-19 in *Pots and Potters: Current Approaches in Ceramic Archaeology*. Ed. P.M. Rice. University of California Institute of Archaeology Monograph, 24. Los Angeles: University of California.
Thompson, R.H.
1958   *Modern Yucatecan Maya Pottery Making*. Society for American Archaeology Memoir, 15. Salt Lake City: The Society for American Archaeology.
Tschopik, H., Jr
1950   'An Andean Ceramic Tradition in Historical Perspective'. *American Antiquity* 15:196-218.
Tufnell, O.
1953   *Lachish 3: The Iron Age*. London: Oxford University Press.
Tufnell, O., C.H. Inge, and L. Harding
1940   *Lachish 2: The Fosse Temple*. London: Oxford University Press.
Tufnell, O. *et al.*
1958   *Lachish 4: The Bronze Age*. London: Oxford University Press.
Ussishkin, D.
1976   'Royal Judean Storage Jars and Private Seal Impressions'. *Bulletin of the American Schools of Oriental Research* 223:1-13.
1977   'The Destruction of Lachish by Sennacherib and the Dating of the Royal Judean Storage Jars'. *Tel Aviv* 4:28-60.
1978   'Excavations at Tel Lachish—1973–1977: Preliminary Report'. *Tel Aviv* 5:1-97.
1983   'Excavations at Tel Lachish 1978–1983: Second Preliminary Report'. *Tel Aviv* 10:97-175.
Van Beek, G.W.
1977   'Tel Gamma 1975–1976'. *Israel Exploration Journal* 27:171-76.
1983   'Digging up Tell Jemmeh'. *Archaeology* 36:12-19.
1981   'Ceramic Exchange and Manufacture: A "Flow Structure" Approach'. Pp. 361-86 in *Production and Distribution: A Ceramic Viewpoint*. Ed. H. Howard and E.L. Morris. BAR International Series, 120. Oxford: British Archaeological Reports.
1984   'Pottery Manufacture: Some Complications for the Study of Trade'. Pp. 55-70 in *Pots and Potters: Current Approaches in Ceramic Archaeology*. Ed. P.M. Rice. University of California Institute of Archaeology Monograph, 24. Los Angeles: University of California.
Vaux, R. de
1955   'Les fouilles de Tell el-Far'ah, près de Naplouse, cinquième campagne: Rapport préliminaire'. *Revue Biblique* 62:541-89.
1965   *Ancient Israel*, vol. 1. *Social Institutions*. New York: McGraw-Hill.
Vossen, R.
1984   'Towards Building Models of Traditional Trade in Ceramics: Case Studies from Spain and Morocco'. Pp. 339-97 in *The Many Dimen-*

sions of Pottery: Ceramics in Archaeology and Anthropology. Ed. S.E. van der Leeuw and A.C. Pritchard. Universiteit van Amsterdam Albert Egges van Griffen Instituut voor Prae- en Protohistorie Cingvla, 7. Amsterdam: Universiteit van Amsterdam.

Vossen, R., and W. Ebert
1986   *Marokkanische Töpferei, Töpferorte und -zentren: Eine Landesaufnahme (1980)*. Bonn: Rudolf Habelt.

Voyatzoglou, M.
1973   'The Potters of Thrapsano'. *Ceramic Review* 24:13-16.
1974   'The Jar Makers of Thrapsano in Crete'. *Expedition* 16/2:18-24.

Warren, H.
1969   'Tonque: One Pueblo's Glaze Pottery Industry Dominated Middle Rio Grande Commerce'. *Ex Palacio* 76:36-42.

Watson, P.J.
1980   'The Theory and Practice of Ethnoarcheology with Special Reference to the Near East'. *Paléorient* 6:55-64.

Weigand, P.C.
1969   *Modern Huichol Ceramics*. University Museum Mesoamerican Studies. Carbondale: Southern Illinois University.

Welten, P.
1969   *Die Königs-Stempel*. Wiesbaden: Harrassowitz.
1983   'The Furnace Versus the Goat. The Pyrotechnologic Industries and Mediterranean Deforestation in Antiquity'. *Journal of Field Archaeology* 10:445-52.

Whitaker, I., and E. Whitaker
1978   *A Potter's Mexico*. Albuquerque: University of New Mexico Press.

Wissler, C.
1946   'Man and his Baggage'. *Natural History* 55:324-30.

Wood, B.G.
1982   'The Stratigraphic Relationship of Local and Imported Bichrome Ware at Megiddo'. *Levant* 14:73-79.
1985   'Palestinian Pottery of the Late Bronze Age: An Investigation of the Terminal LB IIB Phase'. Ph.D. dissertation, University of Toronto. Ann Arbor, MI: University Microfilms.
1987   'Egyptian Amphorae of the New Kingdom and Ramesside Periods'. *Biblical Archaeologist* 50:75-83.

Wright, G.R.H.
1983   'Sausage Shaped Clay Objects—No Problem?' *Zeitschrift für Assyriologie* 73:121-25.
1985   *Ancient Building in South Syria and Palestine*. Leiden: Brill.

Wylie, A.
1985   'The Reaction against Analogy'. Pp. 63-111 in *Advances in Archaeological Method and Theory*, vol. 8. Ed. M.B. Schiffer. Orlando: Academic.

Xanthoudides, S.
1927   'Some Minoan Potter's-Wheel Discs'. Pp. 111-28 in *Essays in Aegean Archaeology*. Ed. S. Casson. Oxford: Clarendon.

Yadin, Y.
1972   *Hazor, the Head of All Those Kingdoms*. The Schweich Lectures of the British Academy, 1970. London: Oxford University Press.
1974   'Four Epigraphical Queries'. *Israel Exploration Journal* 24:30-36.

1976   'Beer-sheba: The High Place Destroyed by King Josiah'. *Bulletin of the American Schools of Oriental Research* 222:5-17.

Yadin, Y, *et al.*
1958   *Hazor 1: An Account of the First Season of Excavations, 1955.* Jerusalem: Magnes.
1960   *Hazor 2: An Account of the Second Season of Excavations, 1956.* Jerusalem: Magnes.
1961   *Hazor 3-4: An Account of the Third and Fourth Seasons of Excavations, 1957-1958 (Plates).* Jerusalem: Magnes.
1989   *Hazor 3-4: An Account of the Third and Fourth Seasons of Excavations, 1957-1958, Text.* Ed. A. Ben-Tor. Jerusalem: Israel Exploration Society and the Hebrew University.

Yellin, J., and J. Gunneweg
1985   'Provenience of Pottery from Tell Qasile Strata VII, X, XI, and XII'. Pp. 111-17 in *Excavations at Tell Qasile Part Two, the Philistine Sanctuary: Various Finds, the Pottery, Conclusions, Appendixes,* by A. Mazar. *Qedem* 20. Jerusalem: The Hebrew University.
1989   'Instrumental Neutron Activation Analysis and the Origin of Iron I Collared-Rim Jars and Pithoi from Tel Dan'. Pp. 133-41 in *Recent Excavations in Israel: Studies in Iron Age Archaeology.* Ed. S. Gitin and W.G. Dever. Annual of the American Schools of Oriental Research, 49. Winona Lake, IN: Eisenbrauns.

Yon, M.
1981   *Dictionnaire illustré multilingue de la céramique du proche orient ancien.* Lyon: Maison de l'Orient.
1985   'Ateliers et traditions céramiques'. Pp. 103-14 in *Chypre. La vie quotidienne de l'antiquité à nos jours.* Actes du collèque Musée de l'Homme. Paris: CNRS.

Zaccagnini, C.
1983   'Patterns of Mobility among Ancient Near Eastern Craftsmen'. *Journal of Near Eastern Studies* 42:245-64.

Zertal, A.
1989   'The Wedge-Shaped Decorated Bowl and the Origin of the Samaritans'. *Bulletin of the American Schools of Oriental Research* 276:77-84.

INDEX OF AUTHORS

The Sociology of Pottery

JOURNAL FOR THE STUDY OF THE OLD TESTAMENT

Supplement Series